Elbridge Streeter Brooks, Howard Pyle

Storied Holidays

A cycle of historic red-letter days

Elbridge Streeter Brooks, Howard Pyle

Storied Holidays
A cycle of historic red-letter days

ISBN/EAN: 9783337289096

Printed in Europe, USA, Canada, Australia, Japan

Cover: Foto ©Andreas Hilbeck / pixelio.de

More available books at **www.hansebooks.com**

STORIED HOLIDAYS.

A CYCLE OF HISTORIC RED-LETTER DAYS.

BY

E. S. BROOKS,

Author of "Historic Boys;" "Chivalric Days;" &c.

*WITH TWELVE FULL-PAGE ILLUSTRATIONS
BY HOWARD PYLE.*

LONDON:
BLACKIE & SON, 49 & 50 OLD BAILEY, E.C.
GLASGOW, EDINBURGH, AND DUBLIN.
1889.

PREFACE.

There never was a holiday but had its store of stories that might be told—if only the heroes and heroines thereof could find audience or opportunity.

We always remember what occurred on special or "holy" days, as they were once called,—more readily than the doings upon days not special. What boy or girl does not hold Christmas day or New Year's day as the brightest of red-letter days?

So here you have the storied holidays of the year —a whole cycle of the best-known red-letter days, in connection with which the boys and girls of the past had happenings that have become historic.

The customs of the days described have been carefully studied, and it is hoped that the frolics and the worries of the real boys and girls here set down may interest those other real boys and girls of to-day who may read of them, and to whom the author gratefully and lovingly dedicates this book.

CONTENTS.

CHRISTMAS.
	PAGE
MASTER SANDY'S SNAPDRAGON,	13

NEW YEAR'S DAY.
MISTRESS MARGERYS' PIN-MONEY,	33

ST. VALENTINE'S DAY.
MR. PEPYS' VALENTINE,	53

ST. PATRICK'S DAY.
THE LAST OF THE GERALDINES,	71

APRIL FOOL'S DAY.
DICCON, THE FOOT-BOY, AND THE WISE FOOLS OF GOTHAM,	91

MAY DAY.
THE LADY OCTAVIA'S GARLAND,	111

MIDSUMMER EVE.
THE LITTLE LADY OF ENGLAND,	129

INDEPENDENCE DAY.

	PAGE
WHEN GEORGE THE THIRD WAS KING, ...	149

A GREAT OLYMPIAD.

THE DAUGHTER OF DAICLES, ... 173

MICHAELMAS.

THE LITTLE LORD KEEPER'S GOOSE, ... 191

HALLOW E'EN.

THE LITTLE DONNA JUANA, ... 211

THANKSGIVING DAY.

PATEM'S SALMAGUNDI, ... 233

ILLUSTRATIONS.

	PAGE
Prince Charles sprang to his side: "If he goes, so do I!"	*Frontis.*
Was this . . . King Henry's self? Margery dropped to her knee,	46
Young William Penn meets the disapproval of his father, the admiral,	62
On the great Terrace of Donegal Castle,	71
"To sea in a bowl!" exclaimed the puzzled Pembroke,	103
The Young Emperor's entrance to the Circus Maximus,	122
The dark and shadowy outline of a man,	140
"A great day this, my young friend," said Mr. John Adams of Massachusetts,	156
"'Tis an unfair race, O master," cried Ephialtes,	185
"Come hither, lads," she said,	201
Surprised by the Hero of seventy fights—the good Lord James of Douglas,	219
The boys present the Salmagundi to the Heer Governor Stuyvesant,	248

I.
CHRISTMAS
A.D. 1611.

STORIED HOLIDAYS.

I.

MASTER SANDYS' SNAPDRAGON.

*[A Christmas Day story of the revel at King James'
court, and how the little Prince Charles fared
with the Lucky Raisin.* A. D. 1611.]

THERE was just enough of December in the air and of May in the sky to make the Yule-tide of the year of grace 1611 a time of pleasure and delight to every boy and girl in "Merrie England" from the princely children in stately Whitehall to the humblest pot-boy and scullery girl in the hall of the country squire.

And in the palace at Whitehall even the cares of state gave place to the sports of this happy season. For that " Most High and Mighty Prince James, by the Grace of God King of Great Britain,

France and Ireland "— as you will find him styled in your copy of the Old Version, or what is known as " King James' Bible " — loved the Christmas festivities, cranky, crabbed and crusty though he was. And this year he felt especially gracious. For now, first since the terror of the Guy Fawkes plot, did the timid king feel secure on his throne; the translation of the Bible, on which so many learned men had been for years engaged, had just been issued from the press of Master Robert Baker; and, lastly, much profit was coming into the royal treasury from the new lands in the Indies and across the sea.

So it was to be a Merry Christmas in the palace at Whitehall. Great were the preparations for its celebration, and the Lord Henry, the handsome, wise and popular young Prince of Wales, whom men hoped some day to hail as King Henry of England, was to take part in a jolly Christmas mask, in which, too, even the little Prince Charles was to perform for the edification of the court when the mask should be shown in the new and gorgeous banqueting hall of the palace.

And to-night it was Christmas Eve. The little Prince Charles and the Princess Elizabeth could scarcely wait for the morrow, so impatient were they to see all the grand devisings that were in store for them. So good Master Sandys, under-tutor to the Prince, proposed to wise Archie Armstrong, the King's jester, that they play at snapdragon for the children in the royal nursery.

The Prince and Princess clamored for the promised game at once, and soon the flicker from the flaming bowl lighted up the darkened nursery as, around the witch-like caldron, they watched their opportunity to snatch the lucky raisin. The room rang so loudly with fun and laughter that even the King himself, big of head and rickety of legs, shambled in good-humoredly to join in the sport that was giving so much pleasure to the royal boy he so dearly loved, and whom he always called "Baby Charles."

But what *was* snapdragon, you ask? A simple game enough, but dear for many and many a year to English children. A broad and shallow bowl or dish half-filled with blazing brandy, at the bottom of which lay numerous toothsome raisins — a rare tidbit in those days — and one of these, pierced with a gold button, was known as "the lucky raisin." Then, as the flaming brandy flickered and darted from the yawning bowl, even as did the flaming poison tongues of the cruel dragon that St. George of England conquered so valiantly, each one of the revellers sought to snatch a raisin from the burning bowl without singe or scar. And he who drew out the lucky raisin was winner and champion, and could claim a boon or reward for his superior skill. Rather a dangerous game, perhaps it seems, but folks were rough players in those old days and laughed at a burn or a bruise, taking them as part of the fun.

So around Master Sandys' snapdragon danced the royal children, and even the King himself condescended to dip his royal hands in the flames, while Archie Armstrong the jester cried out: "Now fair and softly, brother Jamie, fair and softly, man. There's ne'er a plum in all that plucking so worth the burning as there was in Signor Guy Fawkes his snapdragon when ye proved not to be his lucky raisin." For King's jesters were privileged characters in the old days, and jolly Archie Armstrong could joke with the King on this Guy Fawkes scare as none other dared.

And still no one brought out the lucky raisin, though the Princess Elizabeth's fair arm was scorched and good Master Sandys' peaked beard was singed, and my Lord Montacute had dropped his signet ring in the fiery dragon's mouth, and even His Gracious Majesty the King was nursing one of his royal fingers.

But just as, through the parted arras came young Henry, Prince of Wales, little Prince Charles gave a boyish shout of triumph.

"Hey, huzzoy!" he cried, "'tis mine, 'tis mine! Look, Archie; see, dear dad; I have the lucky raisin! A boon, good folk; a boon for me!" And the excited lad held aloft the lucky raisin in which gleamed the golden button.

"Rarely caught, young York," cried Prince Henry, clapping his hands in applause. "I came in right good time, did I not, to give you luck, little brother? And now, what is the boon to be?"

And King James, greatly pleased at whatever his dear "Baby Charles" said or did, echoed his eldest son's question. "Ay, lad, 'twas a rare good dip; so crave your boon. What does my bonny boy desire?"

But the boy hesitated. What was there that a royal prince, indulged as was he, could wish for or desire? He really could think of nothing, and, crossing quickly to his elder brother whom, boy-fashion, he adored, he whispered "Ud's fish, Hal, what *do* I want?"

Prince Henry placed his hand upon his brother's shoulder and looked smilingly into his questioning eyes, and all within the room glanced for a moment at the two lads standing thus.

And they were well worth looking at. Prince Henry of Wales, tall, comely, open-faced and well built, a noble lad of eighteen who called to men's minds, so "rare Ben Jonson" says, the memory of the hero of Agincourt, that other

> thunderbolt of war
> Harry the Fifth, to whom in face you are
> So like, as Fate would have you so in worth;

Prince Charles, royal Duke of York, Knight of the Garter and of the Bath, fair in face and form, an active, manly, daring boy of eleven — the princely brothers made so fair a sight that even the King, jealous and suspicious of Prince Henry's popularity though he was, looked now upon them both with loving eyes. But how those loving eyes would have grown dim with tears could this fickle, selfish, yet indulgent father have foreseen the sad and bitter fates of both his handsome boys.

But, fortunately, such foreknowledge is not for fathers or mothers, whatever their rank or station, and King James' only thought was one of pride in the two brave lads now whispering together in secret conference. And into this he speedily broke.

"Come, come, Baby Charles," he cried, "stand no more parleying, but out and over with the boon ye crave as guerdon for your lucky plum. Ud's fish, lad, out with it : we'd get it for ye though it did rain jeddert staves* here in Whitehall."

*An old English expression equivalent to our modern phrase of "raining cats and dogs" or "pitchforks."

"So please your Grace," said the little Prince, bowing low with true courtier-like grace and suavity, "I will, with your permission, crave my boon as a Christmas favor at wassail time in to-morrow's revels."

And then he passed from the chamber arm-in-arm with his elder brother while the King, chuckling greatly over the lad's show of courtliness and ceremony, went into a learned discussion with my lord of Montacute and Master Sandys as to the origin of the snapdragon, which he, with his customary assumption of deep learning, declared was "but a modern paraphrase, my lord, of the fable which telleth how Dan Hercules did kill the flaming dragon of Hesperia and did then, with the apple of that famous orchard, make a fiery dish of burning apple brandy which he did name 'snapdragon.'"

For King James vi. of Scotland and i. of England was, you see, something too much of what men call a pedant.

Christmas morning rose bright and glorious. A light hoar frost whitened the ground and the keen December air nipped the noses as it hurried the song-notes of the score of little waits who, beneath the windows of the palace sung for Prince Charles their Christmas carol and Christmas *noël:*

> A child this day is born,
> A child of high renown;
> Most worthy of a sceptre,
> A sceptre and a crown.
>
> *Noël, noël, noël,*
> *Noël sing we may,*
> *Because the King of all Kings*
> *Was born this blessed day.*
>
> These tidings shepherds heard
> In field watching their fold,
> Were by an angel unto them
> At night revealed and told.
>
> *Noël, noël, noël,*
> *Noël sing we may,*
> *Because the King of all Kings*
> *Was born this blessed day.*
>
> He brought unto them tidings
> Of gladness and of mirth,
> Which cometh to all people by
> This holy infant's birth.

Noël, noël, noël,
Noël sing we may,
Because the King of all Kings
Was born this blessed day.

The "blessed day" wore on. Gifts and sports filled the happy hours. In the royal banqueting hall the Christmas dinner was royally set and served, and King and Queen and Princes, with attendant nobles and holiday guests, partook of the strong dishes of those old days of hearty appetites.

A shield of brawn with mustard, boyl'd capon, a chine of beef roasted, a neat's tongue roasted, a pig roasted, chewets baked, goose, swan and turkey roasted, a haunch of venison roasted, a pasty of venison, a kid stuffed with pudding, an olive-pye, capons and dowsets, sallats and fricases —

all these and much more, with strong beer and spiced ale to wash the dinner down, crowned the royal board, while the great boar's head and the Christmas pie, borne in with great parade, were placed on the table joyously decked with holly and rosemary and bay. It was a great ceremony — this bringing in of the boar's head. First came an attendant, so the old record tells us, attyr'd in a horseman's coate wth a Boares-speare in his hande; next to him another Huntsman in green, wth a bloody faulchion drawne; next to him two pages in tafatye sarcenet, each of y^{em} wth a messe of mustard; next to whome came hee y^t carried ye Boares-head, crosst wth a greene silke scarfe, by wch hunge ye empty scabbard of ye faulchion wch was carried before him.

After the dinner — the boar's head having been wrestled for by some of the royal yeomen — came the wassail or health-drinking. Then the King said:

" And now, Baby Charles, let us hear the boon ye were to crave of us at wassail as the guerdon for the holder of the lucky raisin in Master Sandys' snapdragon."

And the little eleven-year-old Prince stood up before the company in all his brave attire, glanced at his brother Prince Henry, and then facing the King said boldly:

" I pray you, my father and my liege, grant me as the boon I ask — the freeing of Walter Raleigh."

At this altogether startling and unlooked-for request amazement and consternation appeared on the faces around the royal banqueting board, and the King put down his untasted tankard of spiced ale, while surprise, doubt and anger quickly crossed the royal face. For Sir Walter Raleigh, the favorite of Queen Elizabeth, the lord-proprietor and colonizer of the American colonies, and the sworn foe to Spain had been now close prisoner in the Tower for more than nine years, hated and yet dreaded by this fickle King James who dared not put him to death for fear of the people to whom the name and valor of Raleigh were dear.

"Hoot, chiel!" cried the King at length, spluttering wrathfully in the broadest of his native Scotch as was his habit when angered or surprised. "Ye feckless fou, wha hae put ye to sic a jackanape trick? Dinna ye ken that sic a boon is nae for a laddie like you to meddle wi'? Wha hae put ye to't, I say?"

But ere the young Prince could reply, the stately and solemn-faced ambassador of Spain, the Count of Gondemar, arose in the place of honor he filled as guest of the King.

"My lord King," he said, "I beg your majesty

to bear in memory your pledge to my gracious master, King Philip of Spain, that naught save grave cause should lead you to liberate from just durance that arch enemy of Spain, the Lord Raleigh."

"But you did promise me, my lord," said Prince Charles hastily, "and you have told me that the royal pledge is not to be lightly broken."

"Ma certie, lad," said King James, "ye maun ay learn that there is nae rule wi'out its aicciptions." And then he added, "A pledge to a boy in play, like to ours of yester-eve, Baby Charles, is not to be kept when matters of state conflict." Then turning to the Spanish ambassador he said: "Rest content, my lord count. This recreant Raleigh shall not yet be loosed."

"But, my liege," still persisted the boy prince, "my brother Hal did say—"

The wrath of the King burst out afresh.

"Ay, said you so? Brother Hal, indeed!" he cried. "I thought the wind blew from that quarter," and he angrily faced his eldest son. "So, 'twas you that did urge this foolish boy to work your traitorous purpose in such coward guise."

"My liege," said Prince Henry, rising in his place, "traitor and coward are words I may not calmly hear even from my father and my king. You wrong me foully when you use them thus. For though I do bethink me that the Tower is but a sorry cage in which to keep so grandly plumed a bird as my Lord of Raleigh, I did but seek — "

"Ay, you did but seek to curry favor with the craven crowd," burst out the now thoroughly angry King, always jealous of the popularity of this brave young Prince of Wales. "And am I, sirrah, to be badgered and browbeaten in my own palace by such a thriftless ne'er-do-weel as you, ungrateful boy, who seekest to gain preference with the people in this realm before your liege lord the King? Quit my presence, sirrah, and that instanter, ere that I do send you to spend your Christmas where your great-grandfather, King Henry, bade his astrologer spend his — in the Tower, there to keep company with your fitting comrade Raleigh the traitor!"

Without a word in reply to this outburst, with a son's submission but with a royal dignity, Prince

Henry bent his head before his father's decree and withdrew from the table, followed by the gentlemen of his household. But ere he could reach the arrased-doorway, Prince Charles sprang to his side and cried valiantly, " Nay then, if he goes so do I ! 'Twas surely but a Christmas joke and of my own devising. Spoil not our revel, my gracious liege and father, on this of all the year's red-letter days, by turning my thoughtless frolic into such bitter threatening. I did but seek to test the worth of Master Sandys' lucky raisin by asking for as wildly great a boon as might be thought upon. Brother Hal, too, did but give me his advising in joke even as I did seek it. None here, my royal father, would brave your sovereign displeasure by any unknightly or unloyal scheme."

The gentle and dignified words of the young prince — for Charles Stuart, though despicable as a king, was ever loving and loyal as a friend — were as oil upon the troubled waters. The ruffled temper of the Ambassador of Spain — who in after years really did work Raleigh's downfall and death — gave place to courtly bows, and the

King's quick anger melted away before the dearly-loved voice of his favorite son.

"Nay, resume your place, son Hal," he said, "and you, gentlemen all, resume your seats, I pray. I too did but jest as did Baby Charles here — a sad young wag I fear me is this same fair prince."

But as, after the wassail, came the Christmas mask in which both princes bore their parts, Prince Charles said to Archie Armstrong, the King's jester,

"Faith, good Archie; now is Master Sandys' snapdragon but a false beast withal, and his lucky raisin is but an evil fruit that pays not for the plucking."

And wise old Archie only wagged his head and answered, "Odd zooks, cousin Charlie, Christmas raisins are not the only fruit that burn the fingers in the plucking, and mayhap you too may live to know that a mettlesome horse never stumbleth but when he is reined."

Poor "cousin Charlie" did not then understand the full meaning of the wise old jester's words, but he did live to learn their full intent. For when, in after years, his people sought to curb his tyrannies with a revolt that ended only with his death upon the scaffold, outside this very banqueting house at Whitehall, Charles Stuart learned all too late that a "mettlesome horse" needed sometimes to be "reined," and heard, too late as well, the stern declaration of the Commons of England that "no chief officer might presume for the future to contrive the enslaving and destruction of the nation with impunity."

But though many a merry and many a happy day had the young Prince Charles before the dark tragedy of his sad and sorry manhood, he lost all faith in lucky raisins. Not for three years did Sir Walter Raleigh obtain release from the Tower, and ere three more years were past his head fell as a forfeit to the stern demands of Spain. And Prince Charles often declared that naught could come from meddling with luck saving burnt fingers, "even," he said, "as came to me that night when I sought a boon for snatching the lucky raisin from good Master Sandys' Christmas Snapdragon."

II.
NEW YEAR'S DAY
A.D. 1518.

II.

MISTRESS MARGERY'S PIN-MONEY.

[*A New Year's Day story of the doings at Sir Thomas More's in Chelsea, and how Mistress Margery More's Pin-Money was worthily disposed of. January* 1, 1518.]

IT was a very happy and an altogether jolly family that exchanged the New Year's greetings in the quaint old house by Thames-water in Chelsea scarce three miles west from London Bridge. There were Sir Thomas, the master, and Madame Alice, the mistress, and as for children there were Margery and Bess and Cicely and little Jack, to say nothing of sprightly young Maggie Giggs, their adopted sister, and all the boys and girls that belonged to the servants and tenantry on Sir Thomas More's estate.

I have called it a quaint old house, and so would you esteem it even in these bewildering days of all sorts of odd styles in houses; but in the days of young Mistress Margery it was quite a new house and quite a wonderful one too — for her father Sir Thomas, who was a great London lawyer, had built his big mansion, with its wide porches and its queer gables, its four broad bay windows, its many casements and its colony of rambling outbuildings, not too far from Temple Bar and yet far enough away from London town to have plenty of "elbow room" and a pleasant stretch of river for his daily ride in his four-oared barge over sparkling Thames-water, from Battersea Reach to the Tower Stairs. All that section is now a part of dense, busy, overgrown and bustling London, and the Thames is no longer the clear and sparkling river of three centuries and a half ago; but the children of wise Sir Thomas More thought but little as to the possible future of the big city so near their home; they wandered delightedly beneath the noble elms, pleased with their stables and their kennels, their rabbit hutches and their breezy "academy" or home schoolroom, and knew no greater delight than to watch at the river-wicket for the dip of the barge oars that heralded the return of their good father from his labors in London town.

And a good father he was. Of all the pictures of those harsh and cruel times of power and of passion, and amid all the sights of the gay court-life and glittering pageants of bluff King Henry's time, there is no fairer picture or more inspiring sight than the glimpses we obtain — now from the letters of the wise Doctor Erasmus, and now from the records of the stately Mr. Roper — of the happy household of Sir Thomas More, the great London lawyer, in the early part of the sixteenth century.

So you may be sure it was a merry and a lively New Year's day, as welcome to the children of "Merrie England" in the year of grace 1518 as is the same bright holiday to the children of greater England in these more peaceful times. The big house in Chelsea rang with the cheery cries and counter cries of "A Happy New Year!" and "God be wi' ye — a Happy New Year to *you!*" while again and again the wintry air echoed the jolly chorus of the children:

> Hag-a manay,
> Trol-a-lol-ay,
> Give us your white bread and none of your gray!

All of which meant that the young folks who sang without, desired New Year's gifts, and were in no wise bashful about calling for the very best. And indeed on that one day of the year — in hall, in cottage and in hovel — the demanding and receiving of gifts formed the chief part of the day's festivities.

Sir Thomas More was no laggard in this regard. Every dependant on his bounty — and there were many of these — had reason to remember with pleasure the good knight's well-freighted "Happy New Year." It was one of the few holidays that he determined to enjoy in the quiet, or the riot perhaps, of his big manor house on the Thames amid his romping girls and boys. Indeed it is on record that though he was high in favor as a councillor of the king — bluff, lavish, haughty, obstinate and tyrannical Harry Tudor whom all England bowed low before as King Henry VIII. — Sir Thomas More did not find the favor of a king so delightful as did most courtiers, but complained again and again that he could scarce get leave to run away for a sight of his wife and children.

"And i' faith, my Meg," he said this very morning to the little ten-year-old daughter he so dearly loved, "I do find these home moments so attractive that I am minded to be less mirthful and open of speech with the King's Grace so that, perchance, he may esteem me at length as but a dull-witted fool and so call me but little to his royal house and presence."

But Mistress Margery stopped his speech with a storm of kisses — for she esteemed her father the best, the greatest and the wisest man in all the world.

"Tilly vally, my father," she cried indignantly, "have done with such nonsense-talk! As if, forsooth, any one could deem you a fool — even should you strive to seem one — you who are wiser than all the world beside; ay, and nobler and grander, too, than even the King's Majesty himself."

"Hoity toity," exclaimed Sir Thomas in great

and apparent horror, "have we a rebel and a traitor even here amid our very rabbit hutches! This is a Tower business surely. Why, Mistress Meg, know you not that it is the highest of high treason even to think of any person as being set above the King's Grace?"

"Ay, my father," answered the little maid slyly, "but this is Utopia, you know, and in Utopia — have not you yourself written it — everything is in more perfection than in this England of ours. And if you are king of home as its father and its head are you not greater and grander than even the King of England himself?"

Now *Utopia* — as you young people who are studying English literature know — was written by Sir Thomas More, and is one of the most remarkable of books. So Mistress Margery's reasoning was but sly flattery and a glorification of good Sir Thomas's best regarded work. He was too modest and gentle a man, however, to take over-much credit to himself and he simply laid his hand tenderly upon his little daughter's fair head and said in a sort of mock protest: "Ah, girl, girl; will you too seek to puff your father up with the tickling vanity of pride and self-glory which are only abject and to be despised? Run now, ere your father is thus disgraced, and see to the New Year's oranges and the well-spiced posset that your mother is preparing. Yet stay, child," he added, "take these two crowns of gold for your rightful pin-money* and know, dearest Meg, that the sooner you have spent this well — as you are wont to do — and the sooner you shall ask me for more, the sooner you will do your father a singular pleassure." †

Now there was a father for any girl to be proud of! But, let me tell you also, girls, that here too was a daughter for any father to be proud of. For

---

* In the old days when pins — which you cannot now do without — were a costly luxury used only by the well-to-do, it was a home-custom for the father of a family to give to his wife and daughters on each New Year's day a certain sum of money to keep them in pins for the year. Folks *could* get along without pins however, and so, very frequently, the money given for pins went for some other comfort, necessity, or pleasure. In time the name of "pin-money" became the regular term for a New Year's money gift and has even come down to our own day as standing for a home gift of money for the personal use of our mothers or daughters. So Mistress Margery More understood it and so she accepted it.

† Sir Thomas' actual words.

Mistress Margery More as you shall read in history, was one of the bright girl figures of the past, who from early childhood to graceful womanhood was both a wonder and a delight to her father, her family and her friends.

But girls will be girls. Even precocity sometimes turns to pranks, and when it has such an abettor as sprightly Maggie Giggs the pranks come easily enough.

The New Year's orange had been "stickt round about with cloves," the girls had with due solemnity eaten their "God cakes"—a curious old-time New Year's pasty—and then Maggie proposed that they should go out on the high road and hear the village children sing for New Year's gifts.

To this Margery at first objected, saying that her father much preferred them to remain within the home-bounds; but Maggie's entreaties at last prevailed. For that mischievous young damsel stood in no great awe of good Sir Thomas' warnings, and it is, indeed, recorded of her that she declared herself as "frequently minded to be faulty for the nonce if only to hear Sir Thomas chide me, he doth it with such gravity and moderation, such love and compassion withal."

So it came to pass that ere long the two little maidens skipped through the lodge gates and along the highway, singing as they went a verse from that grand hymn of the old Roman philosopher Boëthius, who was a favorite author in the home-circle of Sir Thomas More :

> Swift wings have I that truly
>   May mount the heights of Heaven ;
> With these when clothéd duly
>   To my eager soul 'tis given —
> The hateful world despising
>   And e'en the air's control —
> To view, while yet uprising,
>   The clouds beneath me roll.*

But as they skipped and as they sang this quaint and solemn old hymn all Margery's fears as to the wisdom of leaving her home for the highway returned as she saw coming toward them a noisy rabble of boys and men. Some of them carried

---

*This new metrical version of the opening lines of Boëthius' great hymn was made especially for this story by Miss Sarah J. Day.

baskets and some bore "stangs" — or cart-poles — and they all were singing — not the noble old hymn of Boëthius, but a rollicking New Year's song:

> Get up, gude wife, for 'tis New Year's day,
> And we come for our right, and we come for our way,
> As we did in old King Henry his day,
> Sing, fellows, sing; hag-man-ha!
>
> If you go to the black ark, bring me ten marks,
> Ten marks, ten pound, throw it down on the ground; —
> That me and my merry men may have some,
> Sing, fellows, sing; hag-man-ha!

The little girls turned to flee as they spied the approaching danger, but they were sighted and speedily run down.

"Shrine fees, shrine fees," cried their captors; "handsel and shrine fees for St. Giles of Cripplegate!"

Now St. Giles of Cripplegate was one of the accepted saints of the old London rabble and his "handsel and shrine fees" were only other names for money for their own boisterous selves.

"Nay, then, you rude fellows," cried plucky Maggie Giggs, "have off now, or we will have your ears pinioned to your ugly heads for thus stopping noble maidens on the king's highway!"

"Ah-ha-ha! noble maidens forsooth!" laughed their captors, derisively — for these rough London fellows did not know the young Chelsea girls — "hark to the little wench threaten us! Basket them, basket them both!"

And almost before the girls knew what was happening to them they were hustled into the baskets — borne by the mob to carry the women in as were the cart-poles to ride the men on who refused them New Year's money — hoisted "shoulder-high" and taken to the nearest tavern for ransom.

But there they were recognized.

"For the Lord's sake, good fellows," cried the amazed and scandalized host, "leave down these young maidens or, by the mass, it will go sorely with ye all! Good sooth, know ye not who they be? These be the daughters of his worship, Sir Thomas More, the King's Justice."

The boys dropped their prizes soon enough, not caring to risk pinioned ears for the sake of their New Year's fun and without even stopping to claim the sixpence each which was the usual ransom dues. Scurrying away, they soon joined themselves to another crowd which was chasing after a poor old woman.

"Ha! the Judas woman; ho! the red-haired witch," they cried.

Mistress Margery heard the shout and saw the poor woman's peril. And now it was *her* turn to grow indignant. She dashed out upon the highway and, shielding the poor creature, faced her tormentors bravely. "You ruffian boys!" she cried, "what mean such cruelties to this worthy woman."

"A witch, a red-haired witch, a Judas hag,"* rose the cry; "have off your hand, young mistress, or ye shall both go to the ducking stool."

"Nay, she is no witch," cried brave little Margery; "she is Gammer Brinton, the herb-woman, whom we do know full well." And then, remembering the might of her father's name, she added, "Sir Thomas More, the King's Justice, will vouch for her."

* An old English superstition gave Judas red hair, and made it an ill omen to meet any person with red hair on New Year's morning.

But her plan of rescue did not prove entirely successful.

"Ho then," cried one gruff fellow, "it is to his worship that we will drag her for judging, for she hath bewitched young Diccon Crutch with her evil eye and her New Year's over-looking. She must be judged for the ducking stool."

"Nay, then will I go with her," said Margery the champion, "and my father shall judge us both. If Gammer Brinton hath the evil eye then have I too, for sure my hair is not of the darkest — the more shame to you for your foolishness." And soon the whole motley throng was clamoring at the lodge gates.

Margery flew to find her father. She discovered him speedily in his favorite walk before what were known as the New Buildings, where were his chapel, his library and his private gallery. But he was not alone. A portly, handsome young man of twenty-five or thereabout, with ruddy face, "admirably proportioned and with a beard that looked like gold," dressed in a rich costume of velvet and miniver, was walking with Sir Thomas, his arm thrown around his neck, "in friendlie converse and secret counsel." Small Mistress Margery, however, was too full of her own concerns to notice any one save her father.

"O, my father!" she cried, "they have haled Gammer Brinton to thee for a witch to be judged for the ducking stool because she is red-haired and ill-omened for a New Year's day. She is no witch, as you do know, and if she be red-haired, why — "

Sir Thomas looked down in some surprise at this sudden interruption and at the flushed face of his little daughter. But before he could speak, his companion said in a loud and hearty voice, continuing Margery's broken sentence:

"And if she be red-haired, why so be other folk, eh, little wench; is it this you would say?" and he stroked his "golden" beard.

"Pardon, my liege," said perplexed Sir Thomas, "this is my little daughter Margery, who seemeth strangely vexed."

Liege? What — was this burly and loud-voiced gentleman King Henry's self? Mistress Margery dropped to her knee.

WAS THIS KING HENRY'S SELF? MARGERY DROPPED TO HER KNEE.

"Pardon, your grace," she said in pretty confusion. "I did not know that you — but then, gracious sir, methinks the color of one's hair doth no more make one a witch than it doth a king."

"Rightly said, i' faith," cried the king, and then, as one who could be gruff or gracious as the humor suited, he caught the little maiden's hand and strode toward the lodge gate.

"Holo there, ye roysterers," he said in his loudest tones to the amazed rabble, while at the same time he threw a handful of coin among them, "be off with ye; but look ye how you blindly judge one to be witch or wizard from the color of one's hair. For even as this little wench hath said, it doth no more make a witch than it doth a king."

"Huzzoy for Harry Tudor! huzzoy for bold King Hal!" cried the rabble, for every London lad — from page to 'prentice boy — knew the breezy, bluff and commanding young King; "long life and many a happy New Year to your Majesty!"

"But as for you, little one," said the King, when once more in the shade of the New Buildings, "know you not that to harbor a witch is felony in this good realm of ours? I have paid my handsel and may go scot-free; but how will you, who have harbored Gammer Brinton here, pay your fine for being thus privy to a felony?"

"My liege," said wise little Margery, looking into her father's kindly eyes for help to speak aright, "my father, Sir Thomas, hath told me that no one can be hurt by the loss of superfluous goods, for that God looketh upon them even as one would have used them had they not been lost. And as this my pin-money"— here she took the two golden crowns from the purse-bag at her girdle — "which he did give me this New Year's morning might have been lost or ill-spent had I kept it, even so will I now, in payment of this fine for felony — if it be felony to protect the oppressed one — give these two crowns of mine to Gammer Brinton here who needeth them sorely, rather than to the State which needeth them not." And she closed this long and somewhat precocious speech by running straightway to the poor herb-woman and forcing the two golden crowns into her hand.

And King Henry, impetuous and freehanded as

usual, caught up the little maid and kissed her heartily and then capped her gift with two more crowns of gold. And as he walked toward the mansion with Sir Thomas he said: "A wise young wench, Sir Thomas. Cherish her well, for such as she will help upbuild this very realm of England."

Did this fickle and ungrateful king remember his words, I wonder, when scarce seventeen years later he grudgingly gave to this true and loyal daughter the severed head of her noble father from its gory place upon the pikes of London Bridge? I cannot say; but when the happy years at Chelsea had grown into those stormy days that came all too soon — when the brave Sir Thomas More dared to withstand this stubborn King Henry to his face and to die for what he deemed the right — amid all the thronging memories of her bright and joyous girlhood the wise and loving Mistress Margery had no pleasanter recollections than those of such eventful holidays as was this by pleasant Thameswater when she made a New Year's gift of her own pin-money to poor old Gammer Brinton, the herb-woman.

III.
ST. VALENTINE'S DAY
A.D. 1664.

III.

MR. PEPYS' VALENTINE.

[*A St. Valentine's Day Story of how little Betty Pierce drew the famous Mr. Samuel Pepys as her Valentine and what came thereof.* A. D. 1664.]

THERE was expectancy and flutter, a writing of names and a drawing of tell-tale slips all over England and of course the hospitable house of Mr. Secretary Pepys in Seething Lane, Crutched Friars, was no exception. For it was St. Valentine's Eve and the man or woman, the boy or girl who neglected to draw for his or her valentine on this delightful and most mysterious of evenings was no true believer in the power of that wise old Saint and in his special patronage of all true lovers and affectionate friends.

Both young Will Mercer and little Betty Pierce, the surgeon's daughter, were positive about this; and when they met at Mr. Pepys' house in

Crutched Friars they knew just what names they had written and just what names they hoped to draw.

Who Mr. Pepys was, and where was Crutched Friars, I cannot now stop to tell, except that the one kept the most remarkable diary that ever was written, and that the other was in London Town. You will know more of both when you study the history of English literature.

At the especial time of which I write, Mr. Samuel Pepys was not thought of as the writer of a diary but as the clerk of the Acts of the Navy — in the boisterous days when Charles II. was king of England and London was devastated with fire and plague, when Cromwell's bones were dragged from their grave to be brutally treated by men with not one tenth of his genius or his patriotism, and when the Duke of York, under whose guidance and patronage the American colonies began to flourish, was Lord High Admiral of England, and the war with Holland was keeping all England and especially the Navy Department, including Mr. Samuel Pepys, in a flutter and a ferment.

Quite a party was gathered at the house in

Seething Lane, Crutched Friars, on this St. Valentine's Eve and pretty Mistress Pepys, with her bright French face and her laughing eyes made a charming hostess. But Will and Betty were restless enough during all the gossip and talk over the latest court and city news — how my Lady Castlemaine had a little black boy as a page; how Mr. Shakspere's play of "A Midsummer Night's Dream" had been played at the King's Theatre and was voted to be "a most insipid, ridiculous play;" how the Duke of York had taken to wearing a periwig, and how all the world was crowding to see the Dutch giant at Charing Cross, under whose arm Mr. Pepys had walked with his hat on and only to whose eyebrows could a man reach with his finger-tips — all these and many more things the children listened to restlessly and waited impatiently for the drawing of valentines.

But, just as the slips had all been made ready and the drawing was to go forward, up the stairs came Mr. Secretary Pepys with a fine young gentleman, so all the ladies declared, dressed in a half military suit whom most of the company recognized as young Mr. William Penn, the son of Sir William Penn, the Captain Commander. And Mr. Pepys in his usual pompous way told how Mr. Penn had just come over from Dublin, and how he had fought against the Irish rebels and saved the life of the young Earl of Arran in the fight at Carrickfergus Castle.

Even this could scarce withdraw the youngsters from their desires for valentines, although Will Mercer did make a mental comment to ask Mr. Penn before the evening was over about the fight and whether the Irish wore skins and ate their prisoners as Dick Hostler, the surgeon's man, had told him.

Then Mistress Pepys ranged the company in two rows — the gentlemen on one side and the ladies on the other — and bade them come forward in turn and drop the names they had written in the vessels she had set for each — one a great punch bowl which the Duke had given to Mr. Pepys, and the other a Barbary dish that my Lord Sandwich had sent her from Tangiers; and Will stirred up the billets in the ladies' dish and Betty did the same in the gentlemen's, while Mr. Penn, who was quite a scholar and a traveller, told how in the old Roman days there had been just such a lot-drawing during the feast of the Lupercalia and how, too, he had joined in the same play two years before in Paris. "Though much I doubt," said he, "the wisdom of so much folly when graver affairs might be more profitable withal."

"Tush, tush, man," cried pompous Mr. Pepys in his grandest style. "Why talk thus and so? Surely you would not wish to stay this so loving a sport," and he pinched Betty's ear slyly and looked across to sprightly Mistress Pierce, the surgeon's wife, as if to intimate that he hoped to draw her name and have much sport therewith. And Mistress Pierce dropped a stately courtesy and said nothing.

The slips, it was understood, were to be drawn unopened and not to be looked at until St. Valentine's morning, when each swain was expected to call upon his valentine with some appropriate present. Bright-eyed Mistress Pepys reminded them of this rule and then bade them draw, while Mr.

Pepys recited with due effect some verses of that Valentine's Day poem of Master Lydgate's which commences:

> Muse, bid the morn awake.
> Sad winter now declines,
> Each bird doth choose a mate.
> This day's St. Valentine's
> For that good bishop's sake,
> Get up, and let us see,
> What beauty it shall be
> That fortune us assigns.

But even as, with much glee and mock solemnity on the part of the elders and with much real excitement on the part of the children, they drew the love-lots, there came a rousing knock at the street-door, and the voice of an angry man resounded through the house, as he pushed past the servant and came storming up the stairs.

The guests looked puzzled, Will and Betty were surprised into a fresh curiosity, and Mr. Pepys appeared much disturbed. He turned toward young Mr. Penn. "Sure, 'tis Sir William's voice," he said.

Almost as he spoke the door swung open and into the room burst the vice-admiral of England, Sir William Penn, Grand Captain Commander in the King's Navy.

Naturally a hasty man, he was now particularly red-faced and angry-looking. He walked straight across the room to where his son stood, pale but calm.

"So, sir," he burst out, "what fresh nonsense is this I hear? Comes to me scarce an hour back Master Josiah Coal, from Dublin, and telleth me that you did join in with those scurvey Irish Quakers in Cork and dragged from their meeting and haled to the prison as a disturber of the peace. Is this so, son William?"

"It is even so, my father," said the young man.

The angry admiral struck his clinched hand on his sword-hilt. "Beshrew me, but this is a fine to-do," he cried; "and Josiah Coal telleth me," he added, "that you have this very day been foremost in a meeting of these malcontent and pestilent Quakers in this very town. Is this also so?"

"It is even so," again admitted young William.

"Then by all the furies," cried the now enraged admiral, "you are no son of mine. You do disgrace the name of Penn by this conduct. Get you home, sirrah; thence take your clothes and never let me see you more. I will see that I do dispose of my estate to them that please me better, and by the Lord Harry were it not that I care not to disgrace you further before this honorable company I would cudgel you soundly for thus throwing to ruin all your noble chances for success in life."

Good Mr. Pepys hated a scene in his own house.

"Nay, nay, Sir William," he said; "do not thus cast off the young man. I'm sure Mr. Penn will listen to reason and he is, we all do know, a most proper and well-guided young man. Let him think well on the unwisdom of a course that may spoil all his chance of advancement, and he will, I am certain, have done with all this 'thee' and 'thou' business — that will he."

Already the choleric admiral began to regret his hasty words, for he dearly loved this son.

"Well, friend Pepys," he said, "he may 'thee' and 'thou' whomsoever he pleases saving His

Majesty the King, His Grace the Duke, and myself his father. And so far as this keeping of his hat on in the presence of all men, which is, I am advised, another of the be-foolings of these folk, why, he may do that, too, though it doth seem most unmannerly, if but he will uncover in presence of the King, the Duke, and myself. 'Tis not my desire to turn the young man off, if he but save his father from further disgrace."

"Ha, well spoken, Sir William, well spoken," said Mr. Pepys; "and Mr. Penn, I am well advised, will consent to your terms; will you not, young sir?"

The young man looked sadly and wistfully at this father whom he too loved so dearly but for whose love, even, he could not barter his conscience.

"Whoever is in the wrong, friend Samuel," he said, turning to Mr. Pepys, "those who use force for religion can never be in the right, and even for the father whom I honor and revere I may not forget my duty to a higher Father, howeversomuch he may threaten or compel me. As to this same Hat-worship upon which you do insist, I may not, in conscience, remove my hat to any man lest by so doing I do perjure myself, seeming thus to proffer to a human creature the same honor I would give to my Creator. I therefore, who can uncover only to my God, will not do so in homage to any man."

"Not even to the King?" demanded the father.

"Not even to the King," sadly but firmly replied the son.

The wrath of the loyal Admiral burst out afresh at this exhibition of what he believed to be a wicked stubbornness in his son.

"Get you gone, get you gone!" he cried, shaking his fist at the young man; "get you gone for an ungrateful, disloyal, canting heretic! From henceforth you are no son of mine and though you do rot in jail I will not lift hand to help or save you."

Even this dreadful threat did not move young William Penn. Still calm and grave of face he turned toward the door and said, in words that have become almost as historic as the famous declaration of Luther: " My prison shall become

YOUNG WILLIAM PENN MEETS THE DISAPPROVAL OF HIS FATHER, THE ADMIRAL.

my grave before I will budge a jot. For I do owe my conscience to no mortal man."

The Admiral, boiling with rage at this determined stand of his son, burst out with, "Unmannerly varlet, out of my sight!" and, whipping out his sword, he struck his son with the flat blade and, as the record says, "fell upon him and beat him sorely and drove him from the house."

Such of the guests as had not already fled to escape the unpleasantness of this family jar now left the house at once, while Mistress Pepys pouted with mortification and the worthy secretary was greatly annoyed and disturbed.

So the Valentine's Eve party, that was to have been so very jolly, was abruptly broken up. But next morning even the exciting scene of the night before could not drive from Will and Betty the knowledge that this was St. Valentine's Day. They opened the slips they had drawn and, early in the day, the children met at the doorway of the house in Crutched Friars, and Will said to Betty, rather ruefully, "I did draw Mistress Pepys, Betty."

"And I did draw Mr. Pepys, Will," Betty responded, with just a perceptible pout; and then she added, "But I do wonder who did draw my name."

"Not I, Betty," said Will soberly. "Would that I had, for I had devised a rare surprise for you."

Then Betty of course asked, "O, what was it, Will?" but the boy shook his head mysteriously, and only replied, "Faith, 'twill keep till another year, Mistress Betty, for then, I may draw you, don't you see?"

"And what have you gotten for Mistress Pepys, Will?" demanded Betty; whereupon the lad exhibited with much pride what afterward Mr. Pepys noted in his diary as "my wife's name writ upon blue paper in gold letters, done by Will himself, very pretty; and we were both well pleased with it." And this motto accompanied the slip: "*Most courteous and most wise.*"

"And so, Betty Bright," said jovial Mr. Pepys as he came upon Betty awaiting him outside his dressing room, "and so, Betty Bright, you have drawn me for your valentine, eh? Well, little Mistress mine " — and he gave blushing Betty a rousing kiss — "and what would you have me give you as a true-love gift — the fairing-ribbon that I bought last Michaelmas from Covent Garden — or a walk in the Park, perhaps, to see the geese and ganders? Hoity toity, young Mistress! but you have no need to so turn up your little nose at that offering; why, I did yesterday attend the King and the Duke around the Park and they did stay so long a-watching the ganders and geese in the water that the Vice-Chamberlain did well nigh lose his — but there! what care you for state secrets, child; you do care more, i' faith, for comfits and favors just now than for all the Vice-Chamberlains that were ever be-ribboned, eh? Well, then, we will not take the walk a-park; here, little one, this may better serve as thy valentine's humble offer;" and he placed in Betty's hands a pretty basket, neatly trimmed, out of which there popped, as Betty lifted the cover, a white kitten with a pink ribbon around its neck and a black one with a red ribbon, and tied to the basket was also the Valentine's motto: *Be True, be Leal, be Constant.*

Betty was overjoyed with her lovely valentine gift and she gave good Mr. Pepys a most appreciative kiss and hurried home to show her treasures.

But ere she reached her house whom should she meet but poor young Mr. Penn, looking so sad and solemn that Betty remembered the terrible scene of the night before and colored deeply as she dropped a pretty courtesy.

"Nay, nay, little mistress; bend not I pray," said the young Quaker. "Such homage is not for me. Though well I know," he added with that courtliness which, learned in king's palaces in his youth, never forsook the stately old Quaker hero, "well I know that this from you is not so much homage as gentle friendliness, and well I need this, for I am this morning in sore strait and stress, and your kindly young face is opportunely met. And only just now I did bethink me of our meeting last night at friend Pepys' house, and though such vanities are but a sad misuse of

God's time, still I did open the paper and lo — hereon is writ your name — 'Betty Pierce.'"

"And I did draw Mr. Pepys," cried Betty, "and see what he hath given me as his valentine favor," and she opened her basket so that Mr. Penn might see both the kittens, black and white.

"And I have naught to give thee, child," he said, "naught save my goodwill and my loving wish that your life may be all sunshine and all smiles."

Pretty Betty felt really troubled at the melancholy strait of this fair and noble young gentleman, and her generous soul sought for some way to express her sympathy. Her eye caught the motto still tied to Mr. Pepys' gift.

"Good Master Penn," she said as her deft fingers untied the motto, "will you not take this with you as my exchange of favors? I would it were more, sir, but my mother hath often said that even in our intentions doth lie the real value of a gift."

"Thy mother is as wise as charming," said the gallant young Quaker, and then he read the motto.

"Why, 'tis an inspiration, child," he cried with brightening face, "'tis new strength to my troubled spirit: *Be True, be Leal, be Constant.* That will I, little Mistress, for I am well-advised that only to such an one cometh the victory."

And then they parted and Mr. William Penn came no more into Betty's life. But when in later years, Mistress Betty Pierce was grown a fine and gay court lady and heard such strange reports of Mr. Penn, how he remained loyal to the unpopular religion he professed, and how he counted persecution and prison and contempt as but little if he were but true to his convictions — Mistress Betty remembered the meeting on St. Valentine's Day and how she had given to the sad-faced young Quaker cavalier who was to go into history as the friend of five sovereigns of England — the simple and truthful Quaker preacher, the busy and philanthropic Lord Proprietor of the great colony of Pennsylvania — the cheery and helpful motto that she had received with Mr. Pepys' Valentine.

IV.
ST. PATRICK'S DAY
A.D. 1540.

ON THE GREAT TERRACE OF DONEGAL CASTLE.

IV

THE LAST OF THE GERALDINES.

[*A St. Patrick's Day Story of the little Lord Geraldine, and how Brian, the Staghound, kept St. Patrick's Day.* A. D. 1540.]

A HANDSOME and brave-looking little fellow was Gerald Fitzgerald, heir to the great Norman-Irish house of the Geraldines, Baron of Offley and tenth Earl of Kildare, as he stood on the great terrace of Donegal Castle, with one hand shading his eyes from the sun while the other rested upon the shaggy coat of his great Irish staghound, King Brian, who stood mute and watchful beside him.

"They should be here by this, Brian," he said, half in confidence to the great dog that looked up intelligently into the eyes of its young master as he spoke. "Lady Eleanor said that the O'Neill would be at the Abbey gate at high noon, and sure 'tis time some news of his coming reached us. I hope nothing has gone wrong."

Something was always going wrong in the life of this brave-looking little lad. Boy though he was, his fourteen years of life had been filled with trouble and danger. For the great Irish house, of which in this year of Our Lord 1540 he was the acknowledged head, was in sore dispute with the determined and masterful King Henry VIII.

Four centuries before, when the great Earl Strongbow had led the Norman conquest of Ireland, a great domain had been given to this boy's ancestors and the name and power of the Geraldines had been absolute through all the fair lands of Central Ireland. As one of their own bards has sung:

Ye Geraldines! ye Geraldines! how royally ye reigned
O'er Desmond broad, and rich Kildare, and English arts
    disdained.
Your swords made knights, your banners waved, free was
    your bugle call
By Glyn's green slopes, and Dingle's tide, from Barrow's
    banks to Youghal,

> What gorgeous shrines, what brehon lore, what mutual feasts there were
> In and around Maynooth's strong keep and palace-filled Adare!
> But not for rite or feast ye stayed, when friend or kin were pressed,
> And foemen fled when "*Crom-aboo*" bespoke your lance in rest.

Princes by their own might if not in their own right, they became Irish "in all but blood," and were now the helpers and now the foes of English aggression as it suited their lordly wills. I do not deny that as a race they had been robbers and tyrants from the first — but so, too, were all the ancestors of the so-called landed aristocracy of England. So, in fact, if you read history correctly, boys and girls, you will agree were most of our ancestors of six centuries back; but I am afraid we think but little of the crime and sorrow of it all and are moved more by the glitter and romance of lance and casque and banneret than by the despair and degradation of the common people who were the real sufferers in all these old-time feuds and forays.

At the date of our story, however, the Geraldines and the Crown were at deadly odds. It was no small thing to brave the displeasure of King Henry VIII. of England — as many a man and many a woman, too, found to their cost. This poor little lad, who dearly loved a merry time and had no wish for any one's hurt, was the last of his race; father and brother and five uncles — seven Geraldines in all — had, within three years, fallen victims to Henry's wrath and vengeance, and young Gerald, now "titular" Earl of Kildare, was proscribed, attainted and pursued by the vindictive English king who could brook no dispute of his authority and who declared that there could be no security in Ireland "so long as this young traytour and his company were abroad."

And so, wherever the English power could reach, this badgered boy was hunted with a fierce pursuit by those who declared that "the bludde of the Gerroldes must be holy extinct," until, through wastes of bog-land and fen-land, through forest and mountain fastnesses, now hidden in friendly castles, and now in friendlier cabins, carried one day in an innocent-looking basket under the very noses of his vigilant pursuers and, on another, in mean disguises and by secret ways far beyond their bitter hate, the boy had at last reached safe haven among the sea-rocks of Donegal and in the castle of his kinswoman the Lady Eleanor Fitzgerald, wife to the Lord O'Donnell whom the Irish still hailed as Prince of Tyrconnell.

But to-day, in spite of his anxiety and the remembrance of past danger, he was in high spirits. For, from every quarter came hopeful tidings. Ireland, that for years had been torn with feud and faction, seemed united at last in a determined stand against English tyranny. The O'Neills, the O'Donnells, and the O'Briens, great Irish chieftains and rivals for generations, had joined hands in friendly compact against the common foe and all the branches of the great house of Geraldine had taken a solemn vow "to rest not neither to be satisfied, but to live foot in stirrup and hand at sword-hilt" until their lord and chief, Gerald Fitzgerald, had been restored to his rank and estates in the earldom of Kildare.

Importance and the expectation of power are always agreeable to any boy of spirit. His bodyguard of twenty-four young Geraldines, his rank and state as the acknowledged head of his house, and the readiness with which he was made the central figure in all the schemes and plans of the confederated Irish chiefs, caused the lad to feel his importance and to accept the homage accorded him — as would any boy similarly placed.

But in the midst of all this importance and high station he was boy enough to welcome and enjoy a good time and to make the most of every possible chance for fun or for adventure. He loved the wild life among the sea-rocks and water-ways of this far northern corner of Ireland — the land of the O'Donnells, now known as the County Donegal. And he knew the land well; for he and Con O'Donnell, the young heir of his kinsman, had roamed over it at will. Bog and cave, rock and ruin, field and forest, Gerald knew them all, from the spouting cave at Horn Head to the banks of the broad Lough Erne, and from St. Patrick's Purgatory to the Bloody Foreland and the Rock of

Doon. He had speared the leaping salmon in Ballyshannon and, with his tireless Brian, had hunted the stag beneath the shadow of the Silver Mountain.

Neither Dublin town nor his own ancestral castle of Maynooth could, he well knew, offer him the wild excitement of the rough riding around Castle Donegal. And so, when the young O'Donnell broke in upon his watching with a proposal for a dash across country to the foot of Bluestack Hill, even Gerald's anxiety to meet the O'Neill at his coming yielded to the temptation. For a gallop to Bluestack was a glorious ride and one that the lads always enjoyed.

But even before they had climbed the slopes behind the noble castle young Con's fertile brain had conceived a still rarer outing. Why should not the Lord Gerald make a test of fate? It was St. Patrick's Day on the morrow; why not brave the vigil in the Holy Cave that very night?

The Irish boys of those old days were full of superstition and of an implicit belief in signs and omens. Every rock and glen and lake and forest had its special and peculiar witch or fairy; there were saint's wells and penance-places in every part of Ireland; and every great house had its especial ghost or banshee to chill and frighten the very bravest lad. Not a thing happened that was not to be explained as due to some mysterious influence, instead of being traced to some common-sense cause.

Con and Gerald had this superstition quite as much as other Irish boys, and Con's uncanny suggestion of a vigil in the Holy Cave was too dreadfully attractive to be resisted.

"But Con, dear," said Gerald meditatively, as they reined in their horses on the slope that overlooked the whole fair valley of the Eske, "I fear me the omens are against me. For, sure then, I have dreamed for now three nights gone that I was speeding gray Maurice across the Curragh and all without the Cup of Kildare. And d' ye see, 'tis a certain sign that the Geraldine who gallops over the Curragh of Kildare without the golden cup shall be the last of his race."

"Ay, but that is a Lenister omen, my lord, and

cannot hold in Ulster," said Con. " For, as you do know, he who can safely keep the vigil in the Holy Cave on the eve of St. Patrick shall have success in whatsoever he may attempt through the whole year to come."

There was no denying this. The vigil at the Holy Cave was at once decided upon, and both boys were soon galloping across country with Brian at their heels intent upon their venture at Lough Derg.

For in Lough Derg, that lonely Irish lake twenty miles away, shut in by barren moors and heathy hills, and on a rocky island half a mile from shore were some scattering stones scarce worthy the name of cave and known as St. Patrick's Purgatory. Here, so the legends had it, the blessed Patrick, patron saint of Ireland, had done some marvellous deed ages ago, and here, too, were the slabs of rock known as the Seven Penitential Beds to which for many a year pilgrims had come, even as they do now, for healing or penance. Gerald had visited the spot before, but never at such a time, nor on such an errand, and as he pushed from shore in the crazy boat kept there for the use of pilgrims a feeling of awe and uneasiness crept over him that would have dashed the spirits of a less brave lad.

Con, with the horses, remained on the shore, for this vigil must be kept alone, but King Brian took no stock in all this foolishness and dashed into the water after his master. Neither Con nor Gerald could force him back. He clearly did not countenance his young lord's scheme but all the same he was too loyal a follower to desert him.

"Ah well, my lord," cried Con, "sure Brian's but a brute beast and the spell sayeth naught against the likes of such marring the vigil." So Brian followed his master, and when the lad sat down upon one of the Penitential Beds to begin his lonely vigil, the big staghound crouched at his feet and Gerald was glad of his company.

At Con's suggestion Gerald had (to keep away witches and unfriendly spirits) thrust into his jerkin, and above his heart, a sprig of the early white-clover leaf sacred to all Irishmen as St. Patrick's flower, the shamrock, and brave at heart, though full of vague and superstitious dread, he manfully resolved to keep broad awake on his hard stone seat above the deep and dismal hole known as the Holy Well.

A healthy boy is very often a sleepy boy and Gerald was decidedly healthy. A twenty-mile gallop across a hilly country in a strong March wind will induce drowsiness. It was well on toward midnight and the desire for sleep gradually got the better of Gerald's excitement and even of his will; he nodded and dozed, dreaming now of the gray horse of Kildare, and now that he was king of England and was thrusting King Henry into the Holy Well; he could see His Majesty going down, down, down and then — splash! — he woke with a great start and shiver only to find himself in the deep and damp hole known as the Holy Well, beneath the Penitential Stones.

Here *was* a dilemma. What should he do? Con, nearly a mile away, could not hear him; for his shouts in that well-hole were muffled and lost. He could not scale the rocky and slippery walls of the pit; and so, Earl of Kildare and Lord of the Geraldines though he might be, he was securely caged in a highly unattractive and uncomfortable place. He called loudly for help, again and again, but no reply came until at last he heard a whine of sympathy, and looking up he could dimly make out the outlines of his faithful Brian the staghound keeping watch above him.

There was dire dismay among the twenty-four young Geraldines who formed the boy earl's bodyguard when, that night, the O'Neill came riding to the gates of Donegal Castle to meet Lord Geraldine and, behold, no Lord Geraldine was there to meet him. Messengers flew this way and that, but to no avail. And Con O'Donnell was missing too, and so was King Brian the staghound. Then there was a swift mounting of horses, hard riders scoured the country high and low, and on the morning of St. Patrick's Day three of the bodyguard riding, in the early dawn, to the Pilgrim's station on Lough Derg came suddenly upon the tethered horses and the sleeping Con.

Their cry of surprise roused the lad; he sprang to his feet and the situation was soon explained.

Then the four standing on the lake shore shouted to their young lord that the season of vigil was over. But no reply came. Again and again they repeated their calls, but nothing save the distant baying of a dog reached their ears. At last one of the castle riders, impetuous as was every Geraldine and unwilling to wait until another boat had been secured, spurred his horse into the lake and was soon swimming across the half-mile of water that separated him from the isle of Purgatory.

The rocky island was reached at last. Dripping and well-nigh spent the good horse clambered to the shore. Again and again his rider's haloo arose. A faint reply came to the searcher's ears, followed by the loud barking of a hound, and the anxious Geraldine guided by these sounds came at last upon his lord and chief — fast prisoner in a damp and slippery well-hole, while above him stood the faithful Brian keeping watch and ward.

Bridle-rein and harness-chain and the ready coil of rope that every raiding Irish rider carried at his saddle-bow drew the boy from his uncomfortable prison. Back to the shore they pulled and were soon speeding straight for Donegal Castle where prince and noble and a throng of retainers anxiously awaited tidings of the lost heir.

And when he did ride through the castle-gate, so great was the Irish faith in the wisdom and virtue of the vigil he had attempted that all applauded instead of censured him, and sought to find in his fall into the well a special interposition of the good St. Patrick himself to keep the lad awake and thus make his vigil successful.

But, after his welcome was over, Gerald found great news indeed and enough to strengthen his belief in the wisdom of his vigil. The blow against England had been struck. His kinsman Desmond was up and had "begun the dance" in Kilkenny. All the Geraldines of the south were in arms. The clans of Ulster and Connaught would join the young earl in his southern march; James of Scotland, the Emperor of Germany, Francis of France, and His Holiness the Pope, had all pledged support and aid, the English were to be swept into the sea and the Prince O'Neill was to be crowned King of Ireland on the Hill of Tara.

The little Earl felt the Geraldine dash and daring rise high and higher as this news was told. His clear young voice counselled instant action and, ere the week was out, the clans of the O'Donnell and the O'Neill, with Gerald and his brilliant following, were hurrying across the hills and plains of Ulster to join Lord Desmond, raise the standard of revolt over the great castle of the Geraldines at Maynooth, and with a united Ireland drive the English usurpers forever from their shores.

Gillies and gallowglass followed with fiery enthusiasm the banner of "the young Gerrolde," shouting the old Geraldine war-cry of "Cromaboo!" and breathing out vengeance and slaughter against the "Sassanach," or English tyrants, who had forbidden the well-known war-cry and proscribed the great house of which this noble young *flaith*, or chieftain, was now the head. On and on they pressed, across the hills and downs of Ulster until at last they came in sight of the old Bridge of Belahoe just south of the present village of Carrickmacross in the County Meath, and there —

Well, there, alas! the old, old story of Irish warfare was retold. Too impetuous for caution, and too self-contained for wisdom, without waiting for the necessary reinforcements from the other clans, and with, it is to be feared, too much of that treachery within their own ranks which has been so largely the cause of Irish failure, they met the English forces under the personal command of the Lord Deputy himself, and the old record says:

> The Irish army were not able to go into order or array as was meet for them; nor did they take the advice of their chiefs to stand and maintain the battle-ground, but they fled in a scattered and disorderly manner, leaving a great deal of spoil to their enemies.

Mr. Froude says, with what the newspapers would call "ill-concealed sarcasm," that the Irish "fled hopelessly and the coronation of O'Neill at Tara was for a time deferred."

And with them fled young Gerald Fitzgerald, disappointed, downcast, and heart-broken — all his high hopes and great plans destroyed, and more certain than ever that his dream was true and his vigil unprofitable. For days he wandered, a fugitive, among the morasses near the coast, cold, hungry, and forlorn, until finally in sorry plight and with but three attendants he was smuggled on board a small ship, as the record says "having on but a saffronyd shurtt, and bareheaded lyke one of the wild Yresshe."

Thus he escaped to France and for sixteen years he lived there, and in Germany and in Italy, an exile and a wanderer, until after the death of his vindictive enemy King Henry VIII. Then he came back, but changed in every respect — a loyal English subject, a Protestant noble of Queen Elizabeth's court, and with no desire for either Irish supremacy or rebellion. He was restored to his estates and title as Earl of Kildare, but in so far as the old warlike spirit of Irish clansman, chief and leader were concerned, the glory of his race was gone and he was indeed "the last of the Geraldines."

And, as he looked back upon his stormy and perilous boyhood, he was wont to say that, after all, his vigil at the Holy Cave had been successful; for defeat at the Bridge of Belahoe had been the best possible experience for him when success might have spoiled his life. Still, he was wont to declare, the vigil was not his but Brian's; for the faithfulness of the noble dog alone had kept him in heart and hope and made him wakeful and watchful in his peril during the mystic vigil on St. Patrick's Day.

V.
APRIL FOOL'S DAY
A.D. 1215.

V.

DICCON, THE FOOT-BOY, AND THE WISE FOOLS OF GOTHAM.

[An April Fool's Day Story of how the "Wise Fools of Gotham" befooled King John of England. A.D. 1215.]

IT was the first of April in all England and it was, therefore, the first of April in Gotham town. Already the trees of Gotham wood had begun to make their "little show of green," and in the bushes on Gotham moor the welcome notes of the cuckoo had been heard, while in shady nook and sunny dell the anemone, the bluebell and the day's eye, or daisy, earliest of English flowers, proclaimed the nearness of the matchless English spring.

From the earliest times the coming of these first days of April had been celebrated with "unbounded hilarity and jocund sports," so the old records say. It had been the Feast of Venus among the old Roman conquerors, the *Oster-monath*, or Easter month, among their Anglo-Saxon followers; and both Roman and Saxon ways found place in Norman-English customs. So there were sports and rejoicings and all manner of pranks and frolics throughout England on this first of April in the year 1215, including the quiet old town of Gotham in pleasant Nottinghamshire.

And yet it was a sad and sorry time in England, a time of strife and bickering between king and barons — this seventeenth year in the reign of King John of England, the year that gave to the world the great "Magna Charta."

But even though king and barons were at loggerheads the boys and girls of that far-off day loved their play and fun quite as much as do the boys and girls of to-day, and so it came to pass that on this especial first of April, in the year 1215, young Richard, or Diccon as he was called, the foot-boy of Sir Gervaise Pigott of Ratcliffe-upon-Soar, a manor not far away, had come into the straggling old town of Gotham more upon his own business than upon his lord's.

What this business really was, surely no mischief-loving boy who has played April Fool's Day pranks needs to be told. The foot-boys of the thirteenth century, barefooted and bareheaded, in their short, hooded tunics and close-fitting brown trousers, were at heart much like the page-boys of this nineteenth century, and found just about as much time for frolic and sky-larking. They made the most of their brief opportunities, even as do their modern successors, and the good citizens of Gotham, staid and sober yeomen all, could scarce keep pace with the twistings and turnings, the quips and japes and catches of Sir Gervaise Pigott's small foot-boy, Diccon.

It so happened that on this very day King John of England, journeying from Leicester to Nottingham, took it into his royal head to pass through Gotham town. Fleet courser-men announced his coming hours in advance and young Diccon's flow of spirits found a new vent in his anticipations of seeing a king.

John, King of England, was not always a pleasant person to see, as many a boy and many a baron knew to their sorrow. He was a tyrant in every sense of the word, at a time when tyranny was the rule rather than the exception. But he was a picturesque villain withal — such a one as we like to read of at this distance of six hundred and fifty years, but one who, we are very glad to think, lived six hundred and fifty years ago. For he had a pleasant fashion of slicing off, on the slightest provocation, the hands, or the ears, or the noses of those who offended him; and, like the "Mikado" of the comic opera, he took special satisfaction in ordering people to a torture that was "something humorous, like boiling oil or melted lead;" children and graybeards alike felt his wrath; his father, King Henry II., died a victim to his perfidy; his rival and nephew, poor young Prince Arthur of Shakespeare's play, was done to death either by his order or his hand; and he would practice the very refinements of cruelty upon all who crossed his path or interfered with his plans. And, yet, he was courtly in manner, kingly in form and feature, the friend and patron of scholars, clever and full of fun even, when it suited his purpose; a splendid soldier, a finished statesman — "the ablest and most ruthless of all the Plantagenets," not even excepting that hero of mediæval romance — his great but blundering brother Richard I. of England, called the "Lion-Hearted."

So you can readily imagine that the poor people who were his subjects and vassals did not particularly care to fall in his way, especially if their opinions happened to differ from their king's. But not even a tyrant can check a boy's curiosity, and, while the good citizens of Gotham town were trusting that the king would choose some other route to Nottingham, young Diccon the foot-boy was greatly exercised lest he should.

But the boy was to have his wish. Swift courser-men galloped up the one long and straggling street of the mean-looking, low-roofed, thatched and dirt-walled town of Gotham and bade the vassals and liegemen of Gotham prepare for their lord and master the king who would graciously pass through their town and take his way to Nottingham by a short cut across the meadow that bordered Gotham Moor.

At this the yeomen of Gotham were sorely perplexed, and every gaffer and goodman wagged head and tongue in sober and solemn discussion.

"Hey day," said one; "here is a sorry pass. If our lord the king do journey over Gotham meadow, then — so his law doth run — doth Gotham meadow become the king's highway ever after. Now we, I think, my masters, are not minded to part with our meadow so cheaply."

"That are we not," said another. "This same John, our king, hath, so am I told, gotten to himself much spoil of good men's land by such contriving, and we be no true men if we do not stand for our rights and our home-lands."

"But," said a tnird, who as reeve or chief dignitary of the town, felt the possible insecurity of his office in case he opposed the king, "were it not wiser for us, my masters, to do the king's behest and so save, at a small loss of land, our town's privileges and, perchance, our own heads too?"

"Nay, good master reeve," the second speaker replied, "we be franklins and freeholders under favor of Sir Gervaise Pigott, our lord of this manor, and 'tis of our right, under the law, to yield our land to none other man, be he king or yeoman."

The determination to lose nothing of interest and to see whatever is going on has been the natural bent of every active boy that ever pushed his inquisitive way into a crowd of his elders, from the days of the Areopagus at Athens to those of the modern political meeting. No lad but has his share of this spirit. Even the Divine Boy of eighteen centuries ago, missed by his parents, was found by his mother "in the midst of the doctors both hearing them and asking them questions."

So you may be sure our young friend Diccon was on hand when in heated conclave gaffer and goodman, reeve and franklin of Gotham town were perplexed and troubled over the coming of the king and the danger that threatened Gotham meadow.

And it was from Diccon that relief came.

"But why doth not our lord king go rather by Wide-mere pool and Cortlingstoke?" he cried. "Surely then, 'tis a much nigher road to Nottingham and the good fathers of Costock Abbey can give him better fare than you."

The pompous and important reeve held back the cuff he was on the point of visiting upon this young intruder as the wisdom of the boy's suggestion became apparent.

"The young japer speaketh sense for once, my masters," he said; "Costock Abbey doth afford more fitting entertainment than doth our poor town, and the red deer run close by Wide-mere Pool."

So three wise old graybeards of Gotham were despatched posthaste and much against their will to meet the king's officers at the ford of the Soar above the old Saxon town of Loughborough. And with them, though keeping discreetly in the rear, went Diccon the foot-boy, resolved to see a live king and to watch the working of his plan.

The three wise men of Gotham, however, moved all too slowly. For, ere they had reached Kegworth Bridge they saw, on the slopes beyond, the runners and archers of the king's advance while scarce a bow-shot behind appeared the steel casques of the Flemish guards, the green jerkins of the royal archers; and, in the midst of the close array of knights and men-at-arms, of barons and of priests, upon a bay palfrey trapped with housings of gold, they saw the "Majesty of England"— King John himself.

There was no time for delay. Each man pushing his fellow forward in turn, the three Gothamites bowed low before the Earl of Pembroke, the leader of the king's advance. In somewhat quavering and still more blundering words they made known their suggestions of a change of route for their lord the king.

King John happened to be in good humor that morning. Word had come to him from Rome that Pope Innocent would lift the ban of excommunication that had been pronounced against him for his quarrel with the Archbishop of Canterbury and would side with the king against his unruly barons.

So, when the advice of the men of Gotham was reported to him, he saw through their little plan, but he looked upon it as a thing to laugh over, as well as the tribute of fear to his power and might. "Do, then, the churls of Gotham hold their king in such dread," he said with a great laugh, "that they must beg his absence from their scurvy town?

Say to the villains, Pembroke, that though it grieveth him sore to turn aside from Gotham town, the king is minded to accept their guiding, and will, as they do counsel, worry the red deer at Wide-mere pool."

"I crave your grace, lord king," spake out a Nottingham man, an archer of the guard, "but he who bids you hunt the red deer by Wide-mere pool is fool and double fool. I know these wolds of Nottingham and never a red deer nor a fallow either can be found around Wide-mere pool. Trust me, 'tis a trick, lord king — a trick or else they all be fools in Gotham town."

At this the Plantagenet wrath broke out.

"Now, by St. Wulstan," cried the angry monarch, "do they dare to trick me — their king? Holo there, Pembroke, de Mauleon, Burck, ride you straight to Gotham town and fathom this rascal guise. And as for yon old dotards, seize and shackle them all. It shall cost them and their brothers many a mark of gold and many a hand and head if that they have dared to juggle with their lord the king."

"Have a care, lord king," said the cautious Earl of Pembroke, "'twere scarce wise to talk of fine and feud against a baron's manor-town while affairs are in so troublous a state."

"Parley not with me, Earl Pembroke," said the wrathful king, "but ride to Gotham straight. We will bide here until you do return and make our action on your truthful tale." But Diccon, where was he when this storm was raging? He was a boy, and knew when it was wise to make himself scarce. So now, dashing across country, stopping not for horseway nor hedgeway, for brook or hill, he left king and messengers far behind and soon burst in upon the startled goodmen of Gotham town.

His tale was soon told. Dismay filled every face. "What shall we do now?" they asked each other. "'Tis now not a matter of meadow land but of fine and blood." For well they knew the temper of King John of England.

"He called you fools and double fools," cried the panting Diccon. "Sure, 'tis All Fools' day now. Why not play the fool and thus mayhap lead the lord king's wrath a-straying?"

Again the boy's quick wit struck the fancy of the perplexed villagers. It seemed their only chance for safety, and at once a hasty programme of absurdities was arranged, with the nimble young foot-boy as master of ceremonies.

And scarcely had they prepared for their serious pranks when out of Gotham wood and down the grassy hill rode, with their archers and spearmen, the three messengers of the king — William, Earl of Pembroke, de Mauleon the Gascon, and the captain of the Free Lances of Brabant, Walter Burck.

These, as they came down the hill, first saw, gathered around a bush, a half-dozen sober-faced men intently watching a gray-backed cuckoo that sung merrily in the bush.

"Where be the reeve of this your rascal town?" demanded the Earl of Pembroke.

"Nay, masters, hush your question and ride on, ride on, I pray," replied one of the watchers in low tones. "We seek to hedge the cuckoo in this bush and thus to keep him here that he may sing a welcome to our lord the king."

"TO SEA IN A BOWL!" EXCLAIMED THE PUZZLED PEMBROKE.

"Well, here be fools indeed," answered Pembroke in contemptuous tones; "they hope to keep the cuckoo waiting till the king doth come. There is no sense in them; ride we on, my lords." And in much disgust the cavalcade rode down the hill which to this day has borne the name of "The Cuckoo Bush."

But ere they reached its foot they met three wise and solemn-looking graybeards bearing between them a mighty wassail bowl.

"Holo, brothers," cried the roystering Dutchman, Burck, "is this our stirrup cup that you do bring?"

"Nay, hinder us not, gentle masters," said the eldest of the three, "we are for Fairham brook to sail away to sea ere that King John doth come."

"To sea in a bowl!" exclaimed the puzzled Pembroke. "Well, here be three wise men of Gotham with a vengeance, sirs. If that the rest be such as these we shall scarce get fair answer for the king to-day."

Just beyond a patch of woodland on the outskirts of the straggling town the messengers came next upon a throng of men engaged in hauling up to the thatch of a long and low-roofed barn all the lumbering wagons and clumsy carts that the village could boast.

"In the name of St. Hilary the good, what do ye here, dolts?" cried the now excited Earl.

"Noble master," said one of the men from the tail of an especially clumsy ox-wagon, "we seek to keep yon wood from the sun's scorching, so that we may have some shade for the king's highway when His Grace goeth across Gotham meadow."

The Earl turned to his companions in open-mouthed wonder. "Am I mad, my masters, or are these?" he said. "Surely never did I see such a warren of March hares. The fools! To line their barn-tops with wagons to shade a piece of woods! How can one hope for wise talk from such as these?"

So they rode on and, in the very heart of the town, they saw a dozen men and boys standing, some in and some about a pool of muddy water.

"Holo, there, knaves," cried Pembroke, reining in his horse, "is there ne'er a reeve or freeman in this crazy town that can give me decent speech or civil answer?"

"Now, softly, softly, gentle sir," said one — the eldest of the group — "ask us nought till we have drowned this rascal eel."

The Earl lost all patience at this reply and spurring his horse straight into the pool laid about him with his naked sword scattering men and boys in a trice.

"Now, by the swine of St. Anthony," he cried, "but this gait passeth all. Drowning an eel? How can ye drown that which liveth in water?"

"Good master knight," said the spokesman of the group, "within this very eel doth live a murthering enemy of our lord king and thus would we punish him that we may find favor in our lord's eyes when he doth visit our poor town anon." And walking gravely into the pool he plunged the wriggling eel once again beneath the muddy water.

The Earl was speechless with amazement and with a look of wonder on every face the whole cavalcade spurred through the village in search for one wise man.

At last, on a hill just without the town, they saw a group of peasants rolling what looked like solid wagon-wheels down the grassy slope.

"More foolery yet?" queried the puzzled Earl. "Holo there, fellows, what do ye roll down hill?"

"What should we roll but fine fat cheeses, sir?" said one of the men, straightening himself to reply.

The Earl of Pembroke leaped from his horse and seized the man by the throat. "Are ye all madmen here?" he cried, "with your sailing in bowls, and your shading of woods, and drowning eels withal? Tell me now, knave, why are ye rolling cheeses down this grassy hill?"

"And why, save that they may find their way to Nottingham market, noble sir," was the reply. "'Tis a straight way there, and cheeses that can go of their own will should find the town readier than asses that be but wilful brutes, pardie."

This last absurdity capped the climax.

"Ye are the asses, dolt," cried the disgusted Earl; and, turning to his companions, he said, "Here is but waste of the king's good time, my masters. Nor sense nor reason can be gotten from such as these. This Gotham town is but a village of fools withal and not worthy the lord king's note or anger. 'Twas but a fitting act for such as these to send the king on a fool's chase a-hunting the deer where are no deer."

So they rode back, past the cheese rollers, past the villagers who were drowning the eel, past those who were shading the wood from the sun's rays, past those who were going to sea in a bowl, past those who were still striving to hedge the cuckoo in the big bush, and so back to the king at Kegworth Bridge, and Gotham town was free.

For, thanks to the advice of Diccon and the wit of the Gothamites themselves, King John did not visit either wrath or fine upon the town. Crossing the Soar at Kegworth Bridge, his glittering retinue rode on through Cortlingstoke, and Bunny, Ruddington town and down Wilford Hill and through Nottingham gates and so into the old Norman Castle built by his own iron-handed ancestor, William the Conqueror, two centuries and a half before.

King John of England, in June of that same year, faced at Runnymede other determined men who would not be fooled or juggled by a selfish king. Magna Charta, the forerunner of our own great Declaration, was forced from him by his confederated barons and the very next year, on October 18, 1216, he died in the old city of Newark, a defeated and disappointed tyrant.

And as for the men of Gotham — well, each gaffer and goodman of the town prided himself upon the clever way in which he had helped outwit a king. They considered themselves as truly the wise men of Gotham town; and for many a year the fame of their doings lived in England though they were called not the wise men but the wise fools of Gotham.

And in these modern April days that see many a joke and many a prank still played upon the first of the fickle spring month, it is interesting for us to know that April Fools have been made for so many years and that not the least interesting was when in pleasant Nottinghamshire, more than six hundred and fifty years ago, Diccon the foot-boy and the wise fools of Gotham "sold" their lord the king and saved their town from trouble.

VI.
MAY DAY
A.D. 185.

VI.

THE LADY OCTAVIA'S GARLAND.

[A May Day Story of the old Roman Feast of Flora, in the days of the young Emperor Commodus. A. D. 185.]

THERE was bitterness and ill-temper in the house of Claudius Pompeianus, senator of Rome. Both these unlovely traits of mind frequently spring from jealousy, and jealousy comes from selfishness. The Lady Lucilla was the daughter of one emperor and the sister of another. The "sacred fire" had been borne before her in the streets and the seat of honor had been given her at shows and festivals. But now her brother, the young Emperor Commodus, had married the Lady Crispina who thus became Empress of Rome, and the Lady Lucilla felt that, as the children say, "her nose was out of joint." Another woman was to take her place as first lady of the land, and the Lady Lucilla, jealous of her new sister-in-law and angered at her brother, found herself filled with bitter and wicked thoughts as she brooded over the affair in her luxurious home.

That home was a splendid palace on the Cœlian Hill — a noble house with gardened roofs and gleaming marble porticoes. For the Lady Lucilla was the wife of the senator Pompeianus, twice consul of Rome, the friend and confident of her father the great Emperor Marcus Aurelius. But now Marcus Aurelius was dead and in his stead ruled his handsome son, the young Emperor Commodus. And all through the splendid city and to the farthest limits of the mighty empire the word of the boy-emperor was law to millions of subjects.

But Commodus, unlike his glorious father — the best of all the Roman emperors — cared far more for his pleasures than for his duties. He delighted in sports and shows and gorgeous spectacles, and the great city in these first years of his reign was filled with gaiety and pleasure in which high and low, rich and poor, joined with equal ardor. Only in that splendid palace on the Cœlian Hill was there ill-will and bitterness.

And yet there were two persons in that stately home who were not sharers in these hard and wicked feelings. One was the noble Pompeianus, senator of Rome, and the other was the senator's daughter, the sprightly little Lady Octavia.

The senator Pompeianus was the friend and counsellor of the young Emperor Commodus, and the Lady Lucilla knew that her complainings would meet with no sympathy from her noble-minded husband; while as for the little Lady Octavia, she was far too busy with her own concerns to take especial notice of anything wrong about the house. For, now had come the brightest day of all the numerous spring festivals of Rome — the fourth day of the Florialia, the festival in honor of Flora, goddess of flowers and of spring — the beautiful and joyous Roman May-day.

In those old Roman days of mingled splendor and poverty, when all the wealth of the world was in the hands of a few rich and powerful families, every Roman noble had a swarm of followers who looked to him for favor, employment, or patronage. These followers consisted of less wealthy friends, clients or dependents, and slaves, and every morning they thronged the house of their patron to learn his wishes or request his favors. Among the many attendants upon the senator Pompeianus his little daughter Octavia found those ever ready and anxious to serve her. And so, on this bright Mayday morning a throng of boys and girls had gathered in the peristylium or broad inner court of the palace where, amid pillars and porticoes and fragrant shrubbery, the marble fountain played unceasingly. Wreaths and festoons of beautiful flowers and glossy green leaves adorned this marble court, and most of the young people bore flowers or garlands in their hands.

"Faith, my Octavia," said a handsome Roman lad — whose cropped hair and full white robe, or *toga*, showed that he had at last attained the age for which all Roman boys longed and which permitted them to assume the *toga virilis*, or robe of manhood — "faith, my Octavia, 'tis a vile hour to rouse a man from sleep. 'Tis too much like going back to the days of thy grandfather, the Emperor Marcus, when, so have I heard, the best Roman was he who rose the earliest. For me, I like it not."

"Fie on thee, lazy one," said the laughing Octavia, a bright-faced, dark-haired little Roman maiden of thirteen, "canst thou not clear thy sleepy eyes enough to remember that the maid or youth who first hangeth the garland on Flora's altar to-day shall have the most of good fortune till the harvest feast?"

"Ay, so have I heard, Octavia," said the lad lazily. "I do remember that when I was a boy —"

"When thou wast a boy, indeed!" laughed Octavia, merrily. "Hearken but to the graybeard!" she cried, turning to the other young people. "Why, 'tis scarce six months, as we do know, since thou didst leave off the *chlamys* and the golden ball,* and now thou dost talk as if thou hadst long ago offered thy first beard-growth to Apollo — when, as we do know again, that we did watch them burn at the very last Lupercalian

---

* At seventeen, the Roman boys left off the *chlamys*, or short parti-colored mantle and the collar and golden ball that denoted boyhood and assumed the dress of a man.

feast. When thou wast a boy, indeed! No, no, my Quadratus; boast of thy toga and thy cropped hair in the Senate and at the baths, if thou wilt, but not in the house of Pompeianus where all remember that thou wast a boy scarce half a year ago."

And pelting the discomfited young fellow with a great mass of brilliant flowers the merry little lady straightened the golden crescent on her sandals that showed her to be the daughter of a senator and, with a cheery cry of "Come, friends; to Flora's altar!" she led the noisy train through the great rooms of the palace and past the garlanded door-posts to the street without.

But in the palace she had left, black treason was afoot. For, when the young Quadratus, sulky and out of sorts because of the unthinking girl's sport at his assumed manhood, sought the apartments of his patron, the Lady Lucilla, with whom he was an especial favorite, he found her listening to the complainings of one of the younger patricians, the senator Quintianus who, for some real or fancied slight from the boy-emperor, was now in hot and bitter rage against the indignities which, as he affirmed, "the noble ones of Rome were made to suffer at the hands of this young gladiator."*

Those were savage old days notwithstanding all the boasted culture and refinement of the Imperial City. Wicked thoughts led to treasonable designs and these, all too quickly, to desperate deeds. Ere the hour for the games had arrived the three plotters had reached, as Roman conspirators usually reached, the savage determination to kill the boy-monarch that very day and mount, upon his ruin, to the throne of Rome.

It was a desperate resolve, but all three were wealthy and powerful, and Imperial Rome was already sunk so low that money could purchase the favor of the army and the people, while bribes and offices could secure the Senate.

" And what shall be the signal, noble Lucilla, by which I may know when to strike ?" asked the senator Quintianus who was to deal the fatal sword-thrust.

*Commodus was an ardent admirer of the sports of the amphitheatre. Indeed, in his later years he fought as a gladiator in the arena, even styling himself "the new Hercules."

"Why, the Lady Octavia's garland," broke in Quadratus. "'Tis the very thing. She is purposing to fling her choicest garland at the feet of the Emperor as he doth pass into the portico that leadeth to his *suggestus*. Let the fall of the wreath be the signal to strike."

"'Tis well advised," said the Lady Lucilla ; "so let it be."

And thus was this conspiracy of a sister against a brother's life carefully arranged.

Meantime, throughout the city, the May-day festivities grew more and more joyous. In later years this festival of the Florialia grew wicked and boisterous, but in the happier days of those noble ancestors of Commodus known as the Antonines as also in his earlier years, it was still a bright and joyous holiday, suggestive of birds and flowers and the glorious Italian spring.

Even before daybreak the slaves of the citizens and the peasants from the Campagna were bringing in great masses of greens and flowers, busy hands were trimming and festooning door-posts and temples, statues, altars and baths, and everywhere the First of May was joyously ushered in.

The Lady Octavia and her merry companions, loaded down with flowers, danced along the streets with greetings or with saucy words for such other groups of May-day revellers as they met. They twined their garlands around the marble columns of the beautiful little temple of Flora which stood not far from the great Circus Maximus, and laid upon the altar in the temple the fairest of their floral offerings, hoping thus to gain the favor of Flora, the goddess of flowers and of spring The *flamen florialis*, or priest of Flora, who stood at the altar — wearing the tall and conical white cap, trimmed with wool and topped with olive wood, the long white mantle and the olive wreath of his order — received and arranged their offerings, and then youths and maidens, joining hands before the altar, went through the figures of a sort of stately minuet or flower-dance and, as they danced, they sang a joyous hymn in praise of Flora, of flowers and of spring.

And now, through the city, sounded the trumpet peals announcing that the earlier festivities were concluded and that the Emperor was about to open the celebration of the games of the Florialia in the great Circus. For, among the Romans, from the most ancient times, the games of the circus and the amphitheatre were a part of their religious worship. Already a vast throng crowded the Circus Maximus filling the *spectacula*, or tiers of wooden seats, while in the great amphitheatre stood the *factiones*, or throng of ushers and attendants, awaiting the arrival of the young Emperor.

The little Lady Octavia was fully as anxious to witness the games and races as she had been to deck the altar of Flora. The Romans were extravagantly fond of games and spectacles, and surely no well-regulated boy or girl in any age but is on the tip-toe of expectation when any great "show" is announced. And to-day, so Octavia had learned, the knight Mœnius was to ride a trained elephant upon the tight rope, and, after the races, five hundred gladiators were to fight with twenty elephants and a hundred mounted gladiators, and it was even said that, before the games were over, the young Emperor himself would exhibit his wonderful skill as a dart-thrower against a dozen African lions loose in the arena. There was promise of much excitement in all this; the dark-haired little Octavia grew more and more impatient and, with her last and choicest May-day garland in her hand, leaned far over her father's *orchestra*, or senator's box, awaiting the approach of her boy-uncle, the Emperor.

There is another burst of trumpets, the noise of loud hand-clapping is heard, there is the stir of preparation among the waiting *factiones*, the swinging curtains of the imperial *ostia*, or king's doorway, are thrust aside and into the great arena, with glittering standards and sacred relics, with attendant priests, prætorian guards, nobles and officers of state, comes the Imperial lad, Lucius Aurelius Commodus, Emperor of Rome.

The descendant of a line of Roman patricians, nobles, and kings, the son of a regal father and of a beautiful mother, Commodus was a strikingly handsome youth. His "charming countenance" was but the appropriate accompaniment of a trim and finely proportioned body; his eyes were full of fire and animation and his close curling hair was of so golden a hue that as old Herodian, who lived in the time of this young lad, declares "whenever he walked in the sun it glittered like fire, and some conjectured, as he went, that a heavenly lustre came with him into the world, and settled on his head." His long white toga, deep-bordered with the imperial purple, sparkled with jewels; and so, radiantly beautiful, he crossed the broad arena toward the curtained passage that led to the *suggestus*, or imperial box.

As he did so, with a glad cry of "*Ave; Ave Imperator!*" (Hail, all hail to thee, O Emperor) the little Lady Octavia standing erect in her father's box flung her fragrant garland at the feet of her sovereign. Her imperial uncle raised his eyes to the box above him in smiling acknowledgment of his young kinswoman's greeting and, at that instant, there darted from behind the curtains of the passageway the figure of a man, clad only in tunic and sandals. He brandished in his hand a short Spanish sword, and as he confronted the startled emperor at the very entrance of the dark

THE YOUNG EMPEROR'S ENTRANCE TO THE CIRCUS MAXIMUS.

passage, flourishing his sword to strike, he cried in loud and dramatic tones :

" The Senate sends you this ! "

Had he been as sudden and as decided in his actions as were the assassins of Cæsar, two hundred years before, the world would have been spared the recital of the terrible crimes that darkened the later life of Commodus the man by the speedy and certain death of Commodus the boy. But Quintianus the senator was a young man who liked to do things for effect, and he spent so much time in this theatrical flourish of his sword and in the fervid declaiming of his words that, before he could strike, the imperial body-guards had recovered from their surprise, dashed the would-be assassin to the ground and dragged him, a helpless prisoner, within the curtained passageway.

The whole affair was so sudden that few save those near to the imperial box witnessed the attack, and their cries of horror were drowned in the greater noise of the shouting multitude who were still loudly applauding the entry of the boy they so admired.

But poor little Octavia saw it all and she saw, also, that the handsome young Quadratus, who had shared her father's box and told her when to fling her garland, had not only seen but expected it. His excitement when Quinitanus sprang from the passageway; his almost unconscious "strike, man, strike!" when the assassin prolonged his actions; and his desperate cry of "undone! undone!" when his friend was overpowered and dragged away, showed to the bright-witted little girl, as it did also to her horrified father, the good senator Pompeianus, that all this dreadful crime had been planned within the walls of the home palace on the Cœlian Hill.

With a cry of "O, Quadratus, thou! thou also!" the little girl flung herself into her father's arms, and, as the discomfited lad fled in dread and dismay from the box, the senator and his daughter also slowly followed him.

The games in the circus went on as if nothing had happened, but consternation and uneasiness filled the breasts of those who had witnessed their Emperor's narrow escape from death and a feeling of mistrust, of hatred, and of revenge filled the heart of young Commodus.

That very night with guilty haste the Lady Lucilla fled from Rome. But ere the dreadful death prescribed by the old Roman law had been visited upon the assassin Quintianus he confessed the plot, and the death of Quadratus speedily followed. The Lady Lucilla was captured and banished to distant Capri, the beautiful island of grottoes off the coast of Naples. And soon her death, sister of the Emperor though she was, was decreed. Only the unbroken confidence of Commodus saved the life of the venerable Pompeianus the senator, and even the little Lady Octavia had hard work to prove her innocence. "For," said the prætors, or judges, "was not the Lady Octavia's May-day garland, cast at the feet of the Emperor, the signal for this dastard blow?"

History records that from this unsuccessful attempt upon his life dates the downward career of Commodus. The words of Quintianus, "the Senate sends you this!" aroused in him both distrust and dread of the nobles of Rome and, step by step, he was led into the life of tyranny and of crime that has covered his name with infamy and caused him to be remembered, not as the bright-faced and manly son of a noble father, but as the most cruel and degraded of all the wicked Emperors of still more wicked Rome.

But the memory of the old-time May-day, the feast of Flora, the festival of sunshine and of flowers, still lives in these better and brighter days of ours. The May-day gatherings and festivities on pleasant English hill-sides and meadows recall those far-off days of pleasure-loving Rome, when boy and girl, and youth and maid, beautified their homes, trimmed the altars in their churches, and sang and danced under warm Italian skies in welcome and in love, while in the great and crowded Circus a deed of blood and a life of wickedness were all unconsciously brought about by the simple and loving offering of the Lady Octavia's May-day garland.

VII.
MIDSUMMER EVE

A.D. 150.

VII.

THE LITTLE LADY OF ENGLAND.

[*A Story of the Midsummer Eve Superstitions and how the little Princess Margaret tried her Fate.* A. D. 1503.]

INTO that picturesque and hill-broken portion of the island of Britain where England and Scotland touch one another — a section known through centuries of feud and battle as the Scottish Border — there rode, one bright June day in the year 1503, a fair little English Princess.

With a gallant display of spears and armor and of nodding plumes, "with minstrels singing, trumpets and sackbuts playing," so reads the old-time chronicle, "with banners and banderoles waving, coats of arms unrolled to the light of the sun-setting, rich maces in hand and brave horsemen curveting and bounding," this little girl of scarce thirteen rode over the Border. She was the daugher of Henry VII., King of England — the impetuous "Richmond" of Shakespeare's bloody tragedy of *Richard* III.— and sister to the boy who was to be at a later day the strong-willed King Henry VIII. Across the fair hills and vales of England, from Richmond palace, near to London town, this little Princess Margaret had come with a noble following, and under escort of her princely uncle the Earl of Surrey, to distant Scotland to meet the man who was to be her husband — the brave, reckless, chivalrous and knightly Prince of the house of Stuart, James IV., King of Scotland.

A fine thing to be a Royal Princess, and a great King's bride, you say? Yes. But what girl of scarce thirteen would enjoy leaving father and mother behind to go far from home into a strange place and among strange people to spend the rest of her life in a family that had always been unfriendly to her own household? Yet this was the little Princess Margaret's fate. All this display and brilliant progress through her father's kingdom meant only this — only this and the union of two nations that had been at feud for ages. It was the sacrifice of a fair young maid to settle questions of state. And when questions of state were to be settled the desires of royal boys and girls went for naught.

And so out of England she rode. Across the Tweed, and through Berwick gates, and all along the old highway that skirted the sea-cliffs of this wild Borderland, the cavalcade moved on, escorted by "above a thousand of the chivalry of the Scottish Marches to guard the person of their Queen," until toward afternoon it climbed the sharp ascent and crossed the bridge of rock that led to the remarkable fortress of Fast Castle.

Now, of all the wild and uninviting places to which so small a Princess and so gay a company should come, the lonely and sea-beaten tower of Fast Castle was surely the wildest and most uninviting.

Look on your map of Scotland for St. Abb's Head — a bold and lofty promontory of Southeastern Scotland jutting straight out into the German Ocean just north of Berwick town. A mile or so beyond St. Abb's Head, and crowning a mass of rock seventy feet above the sea, there rose, years ago, the walls and towers of a grim and gloomy fortress belonging to a Scottish noble, Sir Patrick Home. This was Fast Castle.

If you wish to know just how gloomy and forbidding a place it was you need only read *The Bride of Lammermoor* — one of the dreariest and yet one of the most interesting and pathetic of all the marvellous tales of Sir Walter Scott. For the "Wolf's Crag" of his story, the ruined tower in which dwelt the sad-hearted Master of Ravenswood, is none other than this same Fast Castle, through whose frowning portal on that fair summer day of 1503 rode the glittering train of the little Princess Margaret — the child-bride of the Scottish king James IV.

And yet, gloomy and unattractive as this ocean castle must have been, its loyal Scotch owner, the Lord Home, had made it so bright and cheerful-looking to do honor to his young guest and future Queen that half its grimness and solitude were forgotten by "the little Lady of England," as she was called.

But as the Princess, resting from her day's journey, sat looking from the high windows of the castle out upon the gleaming waters of the restless German Ocean, she was far from satisfied with her position. She had never yet seen the royal knight who was so soon to be her husband and her King. She had, according to the queer old custom "in Kings' houses," given her hand at Richmond palace to the representative, or proxy, of King James, the princely Earl of Bothwell, and had solemnly declared that, "wittingly and of deliberate mind, having now twelve years completed in age," she did "contract matrimony with the Excellent Prince, James of Scotland, taking him for husband and spouse," and "did all other for him forsake during his and mine lives natural." But you must admit that it was not altogether satisfactory, even to so young a girl to say all this without really seeing the one she was supposed to be saying it to. And so as she sat thus in reverie after the pageant and progress of the day she fell a-wondering what sort of man this King, who was so much older than herself, would be like, and as she thought she grew restless, and as she grew restless she became dissatisfied, until, suddenly, she remembered that it was Midsummer Eve.

The Princess Margaret lived in the days when the religion of the world was largely made up of superstition, and when the customs and manners of men were as odd as their costumes. Everyone was superstitious and the boys and girls, brought up amid the fears and fancies of their elders, were firm believers in fairies and elves and goblins and witches and good and evil spirits. Sickness and health, good luck and ill luck, were always traced to some hidden cause rather than to some sensible reason, and the young folk, then, had as implicit faith in signs and spells and omens and tests of fortune as do the boys and girls of these more enlightened days in such foolish little superstitions as thirteen at the table, or walking under a ladder, or seeing the moon over one's right shoulder.

Indeed, it was one of these very moon-signs that came into the mind of the Princess Margaret as she sat thinking about King James of Scotland and therewith suddenly remembered that it was Midsummer Eve.

Now Midsummer Eve was always a time of especial importance in the old days, though we busier and less light-hearted people of to-day know less about it. For the twenty-fourth of June is, in the church calendar, the feast-day of St. John the Baptist, and the night before is known as the Eve of St. John—or, because it is about the middle of summer, as Midsummer Eve. It was for ages, for some reason, a night given up to all sorts of vigils and tests of fate; and its fires, its fasts and its follies were strange combinations of Pagan and Christian superstitions. The rare June weather that makes life particularly worth living in our green isle of Britain helped on all the out-of-door watchings and frolics which had from the earliest times been the especial business of the young folk of the island from Land's End to John o'Groat's.

The little Princess Margaret was as firm a believer in all the doings of Midsummer Eve as was any little peasant girl in all that North Country. Her young head was crammed with the legends and fables and wonder-stories which minstrels and jesters and mummer-folk and nurse-women had sung or told for her amusement and her heart was full of all the romantic thoughts and fancies that are the peculiar property of all young girls in their early "teens."

And, to tell the truth, she was just a trifle weary of all the monotony of splendor that had attended her during her days of journeying to the North, and, Princess though she was, she felt just the least bit of a wild desire to steal away from it all, if only for a little while, and do something rash and quite un-princess-like.

I can't say I am surprised at this, for, to tell the truth, such times come to all of us, especially if we are young and venturesome, and so I can readily believe that when the Princess slyly whispered her desires to her new friend and companion, the daughter of the great Earl of Morton, that sprightly young damsel should have whispered "all right" in reply and sought an early opportunity of helping the Princess to a Midsummer Eve frolic.

The greater part of the royal escort were lodged in the Abbey of Coldingham some three or four miles away; for Fast Castle was but a small fortress — a fortalice, as it was called — and could shelter but a small portion of so numerous a retinue. But all the countryside from the Castle to the Abbey was closely guarded by Scottish men-at-arms, and just how the Princess and the Lady Catherine could have managed to elude the watchful eyes of the ladies-in-waiting and the castle guards I am sure I cannot imagine. But the Lady Catherine was a shrewd Scotch lassie, even if she was a great Earl's daughter, and she knew how to carry out her ends. Then, too, the ample gowns and cloaks of the time of King Henry VII. were capital disguises for trim young figures and could make even a Royal Princess look like one of the castle maidens, if so the Princess pleased.

And so it came about that the two young girls slipped all unobserved out of the Castle and across the rocky bridge that led to the mainland, feeling in the soft June twilight a sense of freedom and relief, all the more enjoyable because there was just a dash of danger and of fear mingled in their adventure.

They counted the bonfires, or "beltane fires," which are a peculiar feature of the night and which flashed out from many a hill-top while, around them, so the girls knew, rings of young people would be found dancing or striving for the lucky brand which would be borne home, all smoking, to bring good luck throughout the year. And as they watched the fires the little Princess told the Lady Catherine how in her own home-town of London "on this vigil of St. John the Baptist every man's door was shadowed with green birch, and long fennel, St. John's wort, apin, white lilies and such like," and how many "garlands of beautiful flowers and lamps of glass and iron filled with burning oil hung all night before the houses."

Then the Lady Catherine, in her turn, told the Princess how in the North, the good folk kept awake all that Midsummer Night lest, if they fell asleep, their souls would leave their bodies and go travelling off to the very spot where their own deaths should some day occur — at which recital both the girls shivered and vowed they would not sleep that night.

And then they both hunted for the fern seed which, if found on St. John's Eve and placed in the pocket is said to make the owner invisible, and the Princess further declared that her nurse-woman, Somers, had told her that if a maid did but sow hemp seed in a solitary spot on Midsummer Eve and did sing softly,

Hemp seed I sow, hemp seed I hoe,
And he that is my true love come after me and mow —

it was certain to come true, because Nurse Somers had known of maids who had proved it.

So they chattered on, and, studying the heavens for signs of good luck, made out of the fleecy clouds, as the old record spells it, "dragones spyttynge fyre, and hylles flammynge with fyre, and armed men encounterynge," all of which meant signs of brave knights fighting in praise of their ladies' names at noble tournaments. And as they stood thus on a gorse-covered knoll the young moon came out from the clouds and sent its soft beams down into the shadowy valley beneath them.

And just then the Princess was asking, as she had asked a score of times before, "But pray, Lady Kate, just what sort of gentleman is your King James? Is he, in truth, as brave-looking as he is brave-mannered?"

"Ask of the moon," answered her companion gayly. "Surely your Grace must know the way; and lo, yonder is the moon all ready for your asking."

The Princess Margaret *did* know the way, for she was versed in all the odd customs of her day. So she courtesied very politely to the rising moon, kissed her royal hand toward it three times in slow succession, and then making it a most gracious bow she sang prettily:

> All hail to thee, moon, all hail to thee;
> I prithee, good moon, now show to me,
> What sort of man my husband shall be.

There fell a most uncanny stillness over everything as her voice died away and then both the girls were startled into something almost like terror to see rising out of the brush below them the dark and shadowy outline of a man!

"THE DARK AND SHADOWY OUTLINE OF A MAN."

He wore the buff jack, or leathern jerkin, and plumed sellat, or hat, of the Scottish yeomen. His strong arm held lightly the wooden targe and broadaxe, and from his stalwart shoulders drooped the folds of the Stuart tartan.

Surprised and startled at this sudden response to their test of the Midsummer Fates the two girls shrank trembling into the dark shadow of a convenient bush and clung silently to one another. Then the apparition — for such it seemed of course to be — first strode in their direction, halted an instant as if listening and then, turning, passed beyond them and disappeared toward the south. But, as a mellow moonbeam fell across the face turned toward them, both girls caught a full look at his features, and the Lady Catherine, clutching the arm of the Princess, could scarce restrain a cry as she recognized with wonder and amazement the fair face, the dark red hair and beard, and the open, manly brow of her Royal Master, King James IV. of Scotland.

The figure disappeared in the gloom and, still trembling with the excitement of their strange adventure, the two girls with scarce a word, withdrew from their retreat and hurried up to the Castle.

Only the Princess whispered, "How shall mine husband be a yeoman, Lady Kate? Sure 'tis a false omen."

But the answer came solemnly enough from her now sobered companion, "No yeoman he, your Grace. 'Twas the King's own wraith speerin' toward his death-place, as I did tell you of."

You may be certain the two girls were not sorry to find themselves within the Castle gates after their mysterious and awesome adventure, and they even received with meekness and grace the stern reproofs of the Lady Darcy and the strong remonstrances of Lady Home for thus playing the truant, and then went with much ceremony and but little talk " to bedward."

Two days afterward, at Dalkeith Castle, the great stronghold of the Earl of Morton, the young Princess met the King. And as with gentle courtesy and kindly words "the handsomest man in Scotland" saluted the little maid, the Princess

Margaret recognized at once in the curling hair and beard, the glowing complexion and the open, manly face, the mysterious apparition of the sea-rocks at Fast Castle on Midsummer Eve.

Space does not permit to tell of all the marvellous and brilliant display with which the wedding ceremonies in Scotland were preceded and solemnized. It is, as told by that faithful old chronicler who took part in it all — John Young, the Somerset Herald — a most minute and highly interesting description of a splendid series of pageants which culminated, on a fair August day of 1503, in the gorgeous wedding ceremony in the Church of Holyrood at Edinburgh, and in which the central figure of all this pageant and ceremonial was a golden-haired young English Princess of scarce thirteen.

But how the merry King laughed long and heartily as his young bride soon after confided to him the mysterious sight of Midsummer Eve! And then it was all explained, as all such mysteries can be. For this Royal King of Scotland, like all the princes of the Stuart name, dearly loved to disguise himself and, mixing with his people, come as closely as he could to their lives and ways. And so, on this Midsummer Eve he had simply assumed the dress of one of his own yeomen and coming down from Haddington had prowled around the approaches to Fast Castle in hopes to catch a glimpse of the little lass for whom he was waiting, and to overhear what the people themselves had to say of her.

But, all the same, the test came true. For, when Margaret's supposed apparition disappeared, it vanished toward the south. And to the south lay Flodden Field. And on Flodden, ten years afterward, September 9, 1513, the brave King James met his death, fighting from a mistaken sense of honor against the power of his wife's brother — the young King Henry VIII., of England.

The after-life of this young Queen Margaret — one of the most prominent figures in Scottish history — the grandmother of Mary, Queen of Scots, and the ancestress of the Stuart Kings of England — is as painful as it is interesting. And if in later years you should read the story of her life you will not be surprised that in those old days of little education and of universal superstition among both high and low "the little Lady of England" should have accepted as a true omen the supposed apparition that came as the test of her Midsummer fate that fair June night upon the moonlit hillside below the grim sea-fortress of Fast Castle.

VIII.
INDEPENDENCE DAY
A.D. 1776.

VIII.

"WHEN GEORGE THE THIRD WAS KING." *

[*An Independence-Day Story of Philadelphia-town, and how young Joe Nixon celebrated the first Fourth of July on the Eighth.* A. D. 1776.]

PHILADELPHIA in July! Not even the most loyal boy or girl of that good old Quaker town but must admit that Philadelphia in July *is* a hot place.

"Warm and sunshiny," were the words that Mr. John Nixon, in his daily journal for the year 1776, placed against the early days of July, but I am inclined to think that young Joe Nixon was nearer the fact when he called it "broiling hot."

Very possibly, however, this slight exaggeration

---

* How fitly Lord Byron's lines, though written for a different purpose, apply to the first days of the American Republic:

> Years ago
> I was most ready to return a blow
> And would not brook at all this sort of thing,
> In my hot youth — when George the Third was King.

on the part of young Joe was due to the fact that he was very busy and therefore very warm. Not that he had anything of especial importance to do. Not always those who are busiest have the most to do; but you see there was a great deal to hear and see in Philadelphia-town in the early days of July in the year 1776 and young Joe Nixon, like a true boy, felt it his duty to be on hand when anything of importance was on foot.

And so he was continually on the go between his uncle's big house on the Water street, the room of the Committee of Inspection on Second street, the parade ground of the "Quaker Blues" on the city common, and the big brick State House on Chestnut street.

For young Joe Nixon was a privileged character and duly felt his importance. His uncle, Mr. John Nixon, was a member of the Committee of Safety, and better still, young Joe was a particular favorite of Mr. David Rittenhouse who "had charge of the public clock in the State House Square." This put him on good terms with a still more influential acquaintance — the doorkeeper of the Continental Congress, then in daily session in the Assembly chamber of the State House.

Young Joe was a quick-witted lad and like all the rest of the race of boys dearly loved to watch and listen even though he could not always understand. Seated by the side of his friend the doorkeeper, he found it very interesting and sometimes highly exciting to follow the proceedings of the bewigged and earnest gentlemen who were talking, discussing, and sometimes getting quite angry with one another on the floor of the Congress. Joe only knew in a general sort of way what all this talk and discussion meant. But one thing he *was* certain of, as were all the boys and girls in the Colonies — and that was that there was a "jolly row" on hand between the colonies and the King. He knew, too, that away off toward Boston-town there had been two or three fights with the King's soldiers, in which the troops of the Colonies by no means had the worst of it. And he knew, most of all, that it was mightily hard just now for a boy to get hold of anything new or nice to eat or to wear or to play with and that, somehow, this was all the fault of King George the Third, and that the Colonies did not propose to stand this sort of thing any longer.

So he had made the most of his acquaintance with the doorkeeper of the Congress and had witnessed most of the important events that had taken place during that lovely Philadelphia June.

He had looked with all the awe of a small boy of twelve upon the fifty or more gentlemen — the delegates to the Congress — who, representing the thirteen colonies, were ranged in a half-circle on either side of Mr. Hancock, the President. But I think he admired, even more, the "elegant standard, suspended in the Congress Room," over the door of entrance at which he sat with his friend the doorkeeper, and which was "a yellow flag with a lively representation of a rattlesnake in the middle in the attitude of going to strike, and these words underneath: 'Don't tread on me!'"

He had been in the Congress Room so often that he knew most of the delegates by sight and name: that gentleman in the big chair behind the heavy mahogany table and the great silver inkstand — the gentleman with the scarlet coat and the black velvet breeches — was Mr. John Hancock, the President of the Congress — "Rosy John," the tory boys called him, much to young Joe's ireful indignation; that gentleman in the long-waisted white cloth coat, scarlet vest and breeches, and white silk hose, was Mr. Jefferson of Virginia; that gentleman in the long buff coat, and embroidered silk vest was, as of course every Philadelphia boy knew, the great Doctor Franklin; and there, too, were Mr. Adams and Mr. Gerry of Massachusetts, Mr. Sherman of Connecticut, Mr. Clinton of New York, Mr. Stockton of New Jersey, Mr. Carroll of Maryland, Mr. Lee of Virginia, Mr. Rutledge of South Carolina and many others whose faces and whose voices had now grown familiar. Even his boyish mind, thoughtless of the present and careless of the future though it was, had felt the excitement of the moment when on Friday, June 7, Mr. Richard Henry Lee of the Virginia colony had risen in his place and, "amidst breathless silence," had read to the Congress this notable resolution:

"*Resolved*, that these United Colonies are, and of right ought to be, free and independent States, that they are absolved from all allegiance to the British Crown, and that all political connection between them and the State of Great Britain is, and ought to be, totally dissolved."

Then Mr. John Adams of Massachusetts seconded the resolution, Mr. Thomson the secretary, made the official entry in the Journal, the Congress, with but few words, postponed its consideration until the next day and young Joe Nixon adjourned with the delegates, like them, half-dazed and half-jubilant.

So, through the long June days, the Congress argued and debated and hesitated while young Joe Nixon — a true type of the restless Young America that is ever in a hurry for action and results — watched and wished and wondered, not thinking of what might be in the future save that King George was to be thrown overboard and the Colonies were to set up for a Nation.

At last, on June 28, a committee, consisting of Mr. Jefferson of Virginia, Mr. Adams of Massachusetts, Doctor Franklin of Pennsylvania, Mr. Sherman of Connecticut and Mr. Livingstone of New York, presented to the Congress a long paper which young Joe understood was called a Declaration of Independence. And although he thought it was splendid and full of the most mightily strong blows against King George, much to the lad's disgust the Congress did not seem to go into ecstasies over it, but hummed and hawed and deliberated until July 2, when Mr. Lee's original resolution was put to vote, carried by the voice of every colony except New York, and the United Colonies were declared to be Free and Independent States.

Young Joe Nixon, had he dared, would have tossed his little three-cornered hat in air with a loud hurrah, but the gentlemen of the Congress, he thought, seemed strangely quiet about it all. He did not see what their wiser heads comprehended, that the vote of the Congress on that Second of July meant years of struggle against a mighty power — sorrow and privation and, perhaps, after all, only defeat and, to the leaders, the disgraceful death of traitors. He saw only the glowing colors of victory and excitement as young folks are apt to, and as it is right they should.

And yet that very night, as the Congress adjourned, portly Mr. John Adams, with whom the lad was quite a favorite, noticed the ill-concealed exultation of the boy and laying a hand upon his head said to him: " A great day this, my young friend ; a great day is it not ? "

" O, yes sir," replied young Joe with energy, " I'm so glad it passed, sir."

" And so am I, my lad," said Mr. Adams, with almost equal enthusiasm ; " you are a bright and seemly little lad and will not soon forget this day, I'll be bound. So mark my words, my lad. The Second of July, 1776, will be the most memorable day in all the history of America. It will be celebrated ere you grow to manhood, and by succeeding generations, as the great anniversary festival, commemorated as the day of deliverance, by solemn acts of devotion to God Almighty, from one end of the continent to the other, from this time forward for evermore." *

* John Adams' own words.

"A GREAT DAY THIS, MY YOUNG FRIEND," SAID MR. JOHN ADAMS, OF MASSACHUSETTS.

"Yes, sir," said Joe most respectfully. He did not comprehend all the meaning of Mr. Adams' solemn words, but he was quite as confident as was that gentleman that it was a day, the anniversaries of which would mean in future plenty of fun and jubilee.

Good Mother Nixon could get but little work from her Joe on the following morning. And though, in her peaceful Quaker way, she bade him beware of too much glorying in all the strife and warfare that seemed a-foot, I rather suspect that even her placid face flushed with quiet enthusiasm as she besought her boy to remember that right was always right, and that it was nobler and manlier to boldly face whatever might betide than to be as were some men in their Quaker town who, so she said, "loved too much their money and their ease, and did but make conscience a convenience, instead of being sincerely and religiously scrupulous of bearing arms." All of which meant that there were some craven folk in that day of manly protest against tyranny who, to save themselves from annoyance, pretended to be Quakers and "non-combatants," when they were only skulking cowards. And all such every honest Quaker utterly detested.

But young Joe Nixon, too full of the excitement of the moment, paid but little regard to his good mother's words, inasmuch as they did not apply to his case; and, hot and panting, fearful lest he should miss something new, dashed up to the State House and slipped in beside his friend the doorkeeper.

The Congress was already in session. Mr. Jefferson's paper called "the Declaration respecting Independence" had been again taken up for consideration, and was being soberly debated, paragraph by paragraph.

Frequent repetitions had made Joe familiar with some of the phrases in this remarkable paper. Even his young heart beat high as he heard some of those ringing sentences — about all men being created equal and being "endowed with the inalienable rights of life, liberty, and the pursuit of happiness;" how that "whenever any form of government becomes destructive to these ends it is the right of the people to alter or abolish it;" that "the history of the present king of Great Britain is a history of repeated injuries and usurpations;" that "a prince whose character is thus marked by every act which may define a tyrant is unfit to be the ruler of a free people;" that "we must, therefore, hold the British people, as we hold the rest of mankind, enemies in war, in peace friends;" that "we, the representatives of the United States of America in general Congress assembled, appealing to the Supreme Judge of the world for the rectitude of our intentions, do, in the name and by the authority of the good people of these colonies solemnly publish and declare that these united colonies are and of right ought to be free and independent States;" and, lastly, that "for the support of this declaration, with a firm reliance on the protection of Divine Providence, we mutually pledge to each other our lives, our fortunes and our sacred honor."

Joe, as I have said, had felt his young heart glow and his young pulse beat under the enthusiasm of these ringing declarations and all this debating and questioning appeared to him as fearfully slow and faint-hearted; he wondered why, since the Congress had already passed Mr. Lee's resolution of Independence they should so hesitate over Mr. Jefferson's Declaration of Independence; and, quite frequently, he felt compelled to dash out into the hot and sunny street and work off his impatience in a wild and purposeless "go-as-you-please" around what was called "Mr. Rittenhouse's Observatory" in the centre of the square.

The day dragged on and so did the debate. Even Mr. Jefferson lost patience and, confessing that he was "writhing" under all this talk, needed all of Doctor Franklin's philosophy and example to calm him down again. So it is not to be wondered at that, late in the afternoon, Joe Nixon, enthusiastic young patriot though he was, grew wearied with the talk and the delay and determined to go home. But, just as he was leaving the building, there dashed into the State House yard, a big chestnut horse covered with foam and dust. Its rider, a fine, well-built man in dust-stained travelling cloak, sprang from the saddle and, dropping the bridle-rein into Joe's ready hand with a quick "Here, my lad, take my nag to the City Tavern stables, will you?" hurried without further words into the Congress room.

Joe's impatience changed to burning curiosity again and, transferring his panting charge to another ready lad for attention, he too hurried into the hall and asked his friend the doorkeeper who this newcomer might be.

"Why, lad, 'tis Mr. Cæsar Rodney, don't you know," replied the doorkeeper. "The delegate from the Counties upon Delaware* whom they sent for by special post only yesterday, since his colony is divided in action and his vote is needful to carry the Declaration through."

"And did he ride from home to-day?" inquired Joe.

"Surely, boy," said the doorkeeper, "clean from the County of Kent, eighty miles away. 'Twas a gallant day's ride and a fair day's work, for by it is independence won."

---

* Until August, 1776, Delaware was known in the Congress as "The Counties of Newcastle, Kent and Sussex upon Delaware;" after that as "The Delaware State" and in 1792 as the "State of Delaware."

It was even as he said. Rodney's glorious ride secured the vote of Delaware for the Declaration and late that very night of Wednesday, the third of July, by a majority vote of the STATES — as the colonies now called themselves — the immortal paper that we know as the Declaration of Independence passed the Congress.

But before it was handed to the secretary to be engrossed, or copied, so that it might be signed by all the delegates, Mr. Hancock, as president of the Congress, affixed to it his bold signature that we all now know so well. And young Joe Nixon had, actually, to stuff his hat into his mouth to stifle the hurrah that did so want to burst out when Mr. Hancock, rising from his seat, said in his most decided tones:

"There! John Bull can read my name without spectacles. Now let him double the price of my head, for *this* is my defiance." *

Then the Congress adjourned and young Joe went home, completely tired out with the day's

---

* Said to have been his very words on signing the draft of the Declaration. The British government had offered a reward of five thousand pounds for the capture of John Hancock and John Adams.

anxiety and excitement. And, though on that notable night of the Third of July a nation had been born, Philadelphia lay quietly asleep knowing little or nothing of the great happening.

Next day — the first Fourth of July ever specially known to Americans — Joe was about the only privileged character who slipping into the secret session heard, from his seat by the side of his friend the doorkeeper, the order given by Mr. Hancock as president of the Congress that " copies of the Declaration be sent to the several assemblies, conventions, and committees or Councils of Safety, and to the several commanding officers of the Continental troops; that it be proclaimed in each of the United States and at the head of the army."

This was all that was done on the Fourth of July, 1776, as young Joe Nixon could testify. But the printed copies of the Declaration prepared for transmission to the several States and to the army and signed by Mr. Hancock, the president of the Congress, and by Mr. Thomson, the secretary, all bore the heading : "In Congress, July 4, 1776," and thus that date has come down to us, as the one to be especially remembered.

That very night Joe heard, at his uncle's big house on the Water street, that the Committee of Safety in Philadelphia — of which, as I have said, Mr. John Nixon was a member — had ordered that "the Sheriff of Philadelphia read or cause to be read and proclaimed at the State House, in the city of Philadelphia on Monday the 8th day of July instant, at 12 o'clock at noon of this same day, the Declaration of the Representatives of the United States of America, and that he cause all his officers and the constables of the said city to attend to the reading thereof."

Here was a new treat in store for young Joe; and when he learned that the Worshipful Sheriff had designated his uncle, Mr. John Nixon, as the reader, Joe knew that this meant a front seat for him and was appropriately jubilant.

The day came. Monday, the Eighth of July, 1776. "A warm and sunshiny morning" again reads the truthful journal, and twelve o'clock, noon, must have been hot indeed. But not all the heat of a Philadelphia July could wither the ardor of such patriots as young Joe Nixon. He was therefore a very "live" portion of the procession which forming at the hall of the Committee of Inspection in Second street, joined the Committee of Safety at their Lodge, and, to the stirring sounds of fife and drum, marched into the State House square. Out from the rear door of the State House came the Congress and other dignitaries and then, standing upon the balcony of Mr. Rittenhouse's astronomical observatory just south of the State House, Mr. John Nixon in a voice both loud and clear read to the assembled throng the paper which declared the United States of America "Free and Independent."

The reader concluded with the glorious words: "We mutually pledge to each other our lives, our fortunes and our sacred honor," and, as his voice ceased, the listening throng, so the record says, "broke out into cheers and repeated huzzas." Then the Royal arms were torn down from above the seats of the King's Judges in the State House, and Joe, like a wild young Indian, danced frantically around the bonfire which destroyed these "insignia of Royalty."

Again, at five o'clock, the Declaration was read to the troops then present in the town, and the evening was given up to bonfires and fireworks which you may be certain young Joe enjoyed to his full content.

And, peal upon peal, sounding above all the shouts and the hurrahing, rang out loud and clear, at both the noon reading and the night celebration, the joyous clang of the big bell of the State House telling the glad tidings of freedom, as well befitted a bell on whose brazen rim men had read for twenty-four years the almost prophetic motto :

" PROCLAIM LIBERTY THROUGH ALL THE LAND TO ALL THE INHABITANTS THEREOF."

To his dying day Joe Nixon never forgot the glory and exultation of that jubilant first Independence Day — the Eighth of July, 1776.

One other notable scene also lived long in his memory — a day and a date new to many of us who have always supposed that the Declaration of Independence was passed, signed and proclaimed on the Fourth of July. It was the morning of Tuesday, the second of August, that same historic summer of 1776. From his customary seat by the doorkeeper Joe saw Mr. Thomson, the secretary of the Congress, lay upon the President's table a great sheet of parchment. And on this sheet carefully and beautifully copied was the Declaration of Independence. Then, one by one, beginning with Mr. Hancock the president, the delegates to the Congress signed the great paper and by that act sent their names down to posterity — famous and honored forever.

Of the fifty-six signers of the Declaration not all affixed their names to the document on that notable second of August. Absentees and new-comers added their names as they joined the Congress and not until the fourth day of November, 1776, was the last signature affixed.

Names and dates go for but little when a great deed is done. The deed itself is of more importance than either names or dates. But in the light of subsequent events there is both interest and pleasure in re-telling the story, and following out by dates, altogether new to most of us, the real progress of the historic document which made of the British colonists of North America a great and powerful nation.

Instead of one "Fourth of July," you see, there were really four:—The Second of July, upon which Mr. Lee's Resolution of Independence was passed by the Congress; the Third of July, upon which the Declaration itself was passed; the Fourth of July, which witnessed the order for its proclamation; and the Second of August, upon which it was actually signed by the members of the Congress.

The original document to which these names were signed still exists, grown worn and yellow with age; the Liberty Bell that rang out the joyous news of freedom on the sunny noon and the starlit night of the eventful Eighth of July is now cracked and voiceless; the signers themselves are now only names and memories; but their work lives in the power and glory of the great nation which they founded, and every true-hearted girl and boy honours the memory and applauds the courage of those devoted men. And upon each recurring Fourth of July every girl and boy in the United States is as joyous and jubilant a young patriot as was ever young Joe Nixon when with bonfire and rude, old-time fireworks, with hurrah and shout and song he celebrated, in the days when George the Third was king, the first Fourth of July on the Eighth.

IX.
A GREEK OLYMPIAD
B.C. 480.

IX.

THE DAUGHTER OF DAICLES.

[An August Story of the old Greek Festival Days in the Seventy-fifth Olympiad. B. C. 480.]

FOR generations the house of Daicles the Messenian had been famous in the Olympic Games. Since the far-off days of the Seventh Olympiad, when their great ancestor, the first Daicles, had won the sacred olive wreath, father and son had in turn struggled for the lead upon the double race-track, and again and again had they borne away the honors and glory of victory.

But now only one man of the famous family of runners remained. Daicles the Messenian, last of the name, he who had borne off the trophies and triumph of the Seventieth Olympiad, was fast approaching the age when he must retire from the race, and only a little daughter, the dark-haired Demaineta, would succeed to his name.

The Olympic Games were the greatest of all the festivals of ancient Greece. For over a thousand years they were celebrated upon the sacred plains of Elis, in the city of Olympia specially built for that purpose. In the pleasant August days of every fourth year the contests for athletic superiority were waged in the splendid lists and he who was declared victor in the foot race, the chariot race, the wrestling match, the boxing bout, or the quoit throwing, was held in even higher esteem than he who marshalled an army or built a temple to the gods. The fame of these contests was world-wide and great throngs of spectators came to witness them from every part of Greece, and from its rich and scattered colonies. Indeed so important a part in Grecian life did these days of sport occupy that the old Greeks even measured time by their recurrence, and the space of four years that intervened between one season of these Olympic Games and the next was called an Olympiad.

And now it was nearing the season of the Seventy-fifth Olympiad — the month of August in the year known to our calendar as 480 B. C. Across the blue Ægean came rumors of invasion and war, threatened by the Persians whom ten years before the army of the Athenians had defeated on the Plains of Marathon. Xerxes, the young but mighty monarch of the vast Asiatic Empire of Persia, had, it was said, gathered an immense army for the conquering of Greece and had already sent into its cities heralds and ambassadors demanding tribute and submission.

But neither wars nor rumors of wars could stop the great Olympic festival. Through all the states and colonies of Greece the peace-heralds went declaring the "truce of the gods," by which for one month all Grecians and their allies bound themselves to abstain from war and feud, and to send deputations and representatives to join in the games.

And so, while the Amphictyonic Council, or Congress of the States of Greece, was pushing forward its preparations to repel the Persian tyrant, in every town and village of the classic land of Greece preparations were a-foot for participation in the games within the sacred walls of Olympia.

Only in the house of Daicles the Messenian — an unadorned and low-roofed building not far from that street in the city of Sparta known as the Aphetais — was there sorrow and dismay. For, on his low and scarcely comfortable couch lay stretched the stalwart Daicles, suffering from a wounded foot, maimed by a falling tree. Sad and sorry indeed was the stalwart Daicles, for he knew that there was now no possibility of his appearing in the ranks of the noted runners who were entered for the double foot-race which he had hoped to win.

The interior of a Spartan house would suggest neither comfort nor luxury to an English boy or girl reared amid all the wonders and conveniences of this nineteenth century. But there was both health and beauty in its arrangements and its belongings, while its main idea of physical culture and development gave, even to the hard and trying lives of its girls and boys, a certain amount of exercise and freedom that made them sturdy, strong and vigorous young folk, agile in every dance and foremost in every game. Even the girls had this quality as well as the boys. They could run and wrestle, they could leap and swing with an expertness that would shame many a modern athlete, and in not a few home contests among the children of her own quarter of the town had pretty thirteen-year-old Demaineta borne the victor's applause from her boyish rivals.

But to-day the little Spartan maiden seemed especially thoughtful. Neither ball nor swing had any attraction for her, and even the miniature galleys in the favorite Grecian game of *Kottabos* floated unmolested in the brazen bowl. At last throwing aside the ivory dice which she had been idly tossing from hand to hand, she sprang to her feet and saying half aloud, "And yet it might be done," she hastened to her father's side.

"My father," she said with true Spartan directness as she stood respectfully before her father, "why may not I take your place in the games?"

"You, girl," exclaimed the surprised Daicles, "why, how may that be?"

"Does my father forget," said the girl a trifle proudly, "that I did win the olive crown in the girl's foot-race at the last festival of Hera?"

"Can I forget it, my daughter," the pleased father replied, "when I have ever before my eyes the portrait which the Judges did accord in honor of your victory? But," he added, "that was but a girls' race, and do you forget the rule which decrees death to any woman who shall join in the holy race?"

"I do not forget it, my father," the girl replied, "nor do I forget that, as only the Spartan girls, of all the women of Greece, are permitted to cross the Arcadian river * and witness the sacred games, so only may a Spartan girl standing in her father's place run in his stead and win, perhaps, the olive crown, even as she has won it before. And, my father," she added with a touch of the real Spartan pluck and courage, "bid me, I pray you, to run this race, and, after that, if I die, I die."

As the girl unfolded her scheme — a bright one and a very shrewd one too — by which she hoped, without discovery, to run in her father's stead, Daicles the Messenian listened — at first, hostilely, then doubtingly, then waveringly; until at last, even

* The river Alpheus upon which the city of Olympia was built.

in spite of his own misgivings and forebodings, he yielded to her request and gave his consent for her to run in the lists and, at the risk of her own life, uphold her father's honor, name, and fame.

Slowly enough, as it seemed to the anxious Demaineta, the time passed, and now the day of the great festival was near at hand. By many a highway, from the east and south and north, the throng of deputies drew near to the sacred city of Olympia*" — "the fairest spot of Greece."

In solemn state with richest vestments, sacred gifts and imposing escorts, as suited the greatest of Grecian days, the appointed deputies from the cities and colonies of Greece moved in brilliant procession to the lodgings specially prepared for them. And among them came the noble Leonidas, "son of the lion," the seventeenth King of Sparta, who was to depart after the games were over with eight thousand Grecian warriors to hold

---

* This celebrated " City of Games," Olympia, was situated in the western part of the Peloponnesus, or Southern Greece, near the Gulf of Arcadia. You can find it on your map on the north branch of the River Alpheus (now the Rouphia) and just east of the modern town of Pyrgos. Its ruins have been recently discovered and excavated by the German archæologist, Dr. Treu.

the pass of Thermopylæ against the invading Persians. The Congress of the Greeks would have had him go at once, but "no," said Leonidas the king, " rather risk the liberties of Greece than march to battle on these holy days."

Beyond the town and across the winding river rose countless booths and tents in which were lodged the throngs of expectant visitors, while in their special quarters were housed the competitors in the games — runners and wrestlers, quoit throwers and chariot drivers, leapers and boxers — strong and stalwart men, sturdy and wiry boys, with muscles hardened and sinews toughened by long and constant exercise in the gymnasia.

And with them came Daicles the Messenian, entered for the *diaulos*, or double race, and attended only by his little daughter, the dark-haired Demaineta.

The hour of the tests is over. Though suffering agonies from his wounded foot, Daicles the Messenian with that Spartan courage that is historic — a courage that could, if need be, endure without flinching the most terrible pain and the most exhausting trials of endurance — had undergone all the preliminary examinations that always preceded the sacred games. He had gone with the other athletes before the *Hellanodicæ* or Judges of the games, and given proof of his pure Grecian descent and his freedom from stain or crime ; with them he had lain his hands upon the bleeding sacrifices before the altar of Zeus and sworn he was duly qualified to compete in the games by a ten months' course in the gymnasium of Sparta ; but when the next oath was demanded — that he would use no guile in the sacred contest — the honest Daicles managed in someway to evade the oath without the knowledge of the Judges. Then, prepared and anointed for the race he passed with the other competitors to the great *stadium*, or race course, which stretched its elliptical track and its long tiers upon tiers of seats to the right of the templed grove of the *Altis*. The lots for places were drawn, the trumpets sounded, and the herald cried aloud the name and country of each competitor — Ephialtes the Malian, Prodicus the Rhodian, Dixippus the Athenian, Daicles the Messenian, and so on ; and as each competitor, when called, placed his foot upon the *grammē* or starting line the amphitheatre rang with shouts of welcome and of remembrance of past successes.

Again the trumpets sounded and the voice of the herald rang out above the lists: "If any man can challenge any runner here for stain of blood or deed let him now speak or forever keep silent."

There comes no challenge from the waiting throng. Now sounds the final trumpet-peal. It is the signal for the start and away like the wind speed the twenty runners straight-away down the course. All eyes are fixed upon them as, speeding so fast that none may be distinguished, they dash down the track, and no one notes how, as they start, a lithe and slender figure darts out from the shadow of the golden statue of Endymion near to the *aphesis* or starting place and springs into the rank of the race, while the stalwart form of Daicles the Messenian, spent with long concealed pain, drops fainting near the vaulted entrance of the runners just outside the limits of the course.

Down the broad track fly the runners. Six hundred feet away rises the slender column of the *kamptēr* or turning-point. The foremost runners gain it, they turn and speed back toward the starting-point. Now four, now three are even in the race. They pass the middle pillar on the home stretch. Now two only lead, and now the smaller of the two, as if by a sudden spurt, leaps far ahead, dashes up to the starting-point, lays hands upon the pillar of the *aphesis* and sinks to the ground while the vast amphitheatre rings again and again with the shouts of the spectators. Another instant and the hands of Ephialtes the Malian touch the marble pillar — Ephialtes the Malian, a lagging second in the race.

The president or chief of the nine Judges, clad in his *porphuris*, or purple robes of office, rose in his place and took from the hands of the boy, whose duty it was to cut with golden sickle the wreath from the sacred olive tree, the victor's garland and the branch of palm. But, ere he could step down to the base of the marble pillar of the *aphesis* at the foot of which still crouched the panting victor, the *alutarchos* or chief of the police of the games had sprung forward and rudely clutched the short robe or *chiton* of the winner in the race.

An angry clamor filled the air at this apparent sacrilege. For the victor in the *diaulos* at Olympia was esteemed a hero on whom it was worse than treason to lay rough hands. But the president of the Judges started also in amazement and lifted his hands in holy horror as he looked upon the face and form of the shrinking victor whom the chief of police now dragged before him.

" How; a girl ! " he exclaimed.

" Even so, O master," said the scandalized *alutarchos*.

" Unhappy maiden; what sacrilege is this ? " demanded the president. " Speak. Who art thou ? "

And the young girl, now no longer shrinking and fearful, drew herself proudly up and looked her questioner full in the face.

" I am Demaineta," she said, " the daughter of Daicles the Messenian."

" The daughter of Daicles ! " echoed the president. " Then where is he among the runners ? "

"'TIS AN UNFAIR RACE, O MASTER," CRIED EPHIALTES.

"Look not among the runners for Daicles the Messenian," the girl replied; "he lieth in the archway yonder stricken with pain and I did run in his stead to uphold his honor and his name."

"Then, O Master, 'tis an unfair race, and I am winner," said Ephialtes the Malian. "For 'tis our law that no woman may run in the race. I demand judgment. What is her doom?"

And the answer came from the grim *alutarchos*, "Her doom is death. She must be hurled from the Typæan rock."

Then said Ephialtes again, "I demand judgment, O Master. The olive crown is mine; for I am winner in the race. And as for this false daughter of a falser father let her be hurried to the Typæan rock."

But the calm voice of the president said, "This is not for thy settling, O Ephialtes. Let the *Hellanodicæ* decide. Bear the maiden to the council hall and take thither also her father, Daicles the Messenian."

In the *Bouleuterion* or council hall, near to the south wall of the *Altis*, the nine Judges sat in solemn debate. And when they had learned all the facts — the courage of the sick Daicles and the devotion of his heroic child; when they remembered the fleet runner's past triumphs and how both father and daughter sought but to uphold the fame and glory of their ancestors, their denunciations turned to delight and they announced to the people that the daughter of Daicles was clearly entitled to the victor's olive wreath and was worthy of all honor as a noble daughter and a true Spartan maiden.

And Leonidas the king said to the dark-haired girl:

"Would that my eight thousand Grecians were but as thee, O Demaineta. Then should not Xerxes nor all his hosts prevail against me at the pass of Thermopylæ."

Only in the breast of Ephialtes the Malian lurked the twin demons of envy and hate. Angered at the decision against him he straightway left the sacred city of the games, and betook himself to the camp of Xerxes the Persian. And history tells us how after the first great day at Thermopylæ, when the

King Leonidas and his eight thousand men had held the pass against the furious Medes and Cissians of King Xerxes' host, the traitor Ephialtes disclosed to the Persian tyrant the existence of a secret pass over Mount Æta by which they might descend upon the Grecian rear. Then came the second day at Thermopylæ. Leonidas and his three hundred became historic in their glorious deaths, while from that fatal field the name of Ephialtes the Malian has come down to us as that of a dastard and a traitor.

So the olive crown came again to the family of Daicles the Messenian. So in the fair August festival of old Greece did a brave young girl uphold her father's fame and honor. Loyal then in her youth, Demaineta the daughter of Daicles, proved herself a true Spartan in her womanhood; a noble mother who, so the record says, "could see with pride her sons march to battle and repress her grief when they returned no more."

And thus has the old Greek poet made her real to us — the Grecian mother who in the bravery of the girl clearly foreshadowed the courage of the woman :

> Eight sons Demaineta to battle sent,
> And buried all beneath one monument;
> No tear she shed for sorrow, but thus spake :
> " Sparta, I bore these children for thy sake."

X.
MICHAELMAS
A.D. 1574.

X.

THE LITTLE LORD KEEPER'S GOOSE.

[A Michaelmas* Story of young Francis Bacon and "Good Queen Bess." September, 1574.]

THE pleasant county of Hertfordshire is a charming country to live in, and so thought the two Bacon boys, Anthony and Francis. In fact they roundly declared that it was the very best county in all England and that Gorhambury was the very best spot in the whole county. And I am inclined to think that they were not far out of the way in their statement, as any one who knows the hills and vales of Herts and the famous vicinity of Gorhambury House is able to testify.

---

* Michaelmas Day, which falls on September 29th, was one of the regular holy days of the old Church calendar. It has long been known and celebrated as the Festival Day of St. Michael the Archangel, and is thought to be an acknowledgment of the protection of the guardian angels, Michael being the chief of the angels It had in the olden time many quaint and curious customs, and the Michaelmas goose was a feature of the day which has not yet disappeared.

For Gorhambury House was the fine old manor house of the father of these two boys, the grave-faced but fat Sir Nicholas Bacon, Lord Keeper of the Great Seal and Counsellor to Her Majesty, Elizabeth Queen of England.

Both the lads were Cambridge students now, and though Anthony was fifteen and Francis was twelve, the younger boy was much the stronger and more alert of the two. Poor Anthony had always been weak and sickly. Indeed the boys' tutor, Master John Whitgift, declared that he expended more money for medicines " for Anthonie's beeing syck," as the old spelling has it, than for his studies.

But when the boys were at Gorhambury even Anthony brightened up and was out with his brother, on horseback and a-foot, chasing the rabbit and the fox to cover, or fishing in the Ver, near by, for trout or grayling. The boys could show you just where Cæsar had beaten Cassivelaunus the Briton at Verulam, and just where Boadicea the warrior queen had revenged herself upon the Romans—for the country road about their lovely home was storied ground away back to the days of the Danes, of Cæsar and the Druids. But, more than Norman or Dane, Saxon, Roman or British happenings, what especially interested the two lads, on this particular September day in the year 1574, was the fact that they were at home for the Michaelmas feasting and bound to have a jolly good time.

To be sure the Lady Ann, their mother, kept a very strict watch upon their actions, but to-day she was deeply engaged with Doctor Parker upon the translation of a dry old Latin book written by Doctor Jewel, the bishop, and called "an Apologie of the Church of England;" for the Lady Ann was quite a literary woman. And so the boys were determined in some way to hunt out and entrap as good a stubble goose as could be found in Hertford fields for their own and particular Michaelmas dinner on the morrow.

"And let me tell you, Anthony," said young Francis as he tightened the "bewits," or leathern bell-straps on his falcon's legs, "I am not to be put off with some tame barn-yard goose from Gaffer

Hernston's run. I know where the gray lag feeds in the stubble grounds; I did mark the spot yesterday, and where so live a lure doth wait for Donald's stoop, I am bounden to have that or none."

Anthony Bacon gave a nod of assent to his more energetic brother's plans. He had been kept so much from out-of-doors pursuits that he had but little skill in falconry, but, with the willingness of an invalid, he loved to watch young Francis's apt handling of his bird and to share in all the excitement of his success.

Young Francis Bacon was an ardent admirer of the beautiful in nature and in art. His biographer asserts that, " he grew into his teens a grave yet sunny boy, in love with the daisies and the forget-me-nots," and yet equally ready to "course after pigeons which he particularly liked in a pie," and to dote "like a young girl on poetry, gay colors and the trappings of a horse."

And so he could not but be moved with the green slopes and leafy woods of Gorhambury as he and his brother walked briskly on toward the

September stubble-fields near the banks of the lovely Ver.

"Do you know, Anthony lad," he said, as they hurried on, "somehow this day doth remind me of those lines that Master Spenser read to us from his own papers t'other day. I can even remember how they run:

> What more felicitie can fall to creature
> Than to enjoy delight with libertie,
> And to be lord of all the workes of nature,
> To reine in th' aire from earth to higher skie,
> To feed on flowers and weeds of glorious feature."

But, even as he quoted from the lines of the young Cambridge bachelor, or tutor, who was to be in after years one of the greatest of England's poets, the lad did not forget that his main purpose was not verse-reciting but a fine Michaelmas goose. And as he walked and talked he kept a watchful eye toward the stubble field, and held his hand in readiness to loosen Donald's hood and slip his leash.

Donald was a trim young falcon — a tiercel or male goshawk — and a much finer and brighter bird than most of its kind were apt to be. So

Francis Bacon, skilled in falconry, claimed, and so he hoped to prove. The test came soon enough.

"There, Anthony, there; see yon," he whispered, clutching his brother's arm, "what did I tell you? I marked the spot yesterday and there waiteth our Michaelmas goose — as fine and plump a big gray lag as ever ate English stubble."

And Anthony, following the direction of his brother's finger, saw in the mowed or stubble-land that sloped down to the Ver a great goose, of the kind known as the gray lag, eating away for dear life and all unconscious of danger.

Francis at once broke out into a flow of falcon-talk, almost unintelligible to us who know but little of falconry in these later days of dog and gun.

"Now, Donald, now, bird — go!" he cried, as he unhooded the trim young tiercel and slipped the leash that had held it to his wrist; "bate, bird, bate!" he added, and the well-trained goshawk shot upward into the air and poised high above the game, or "quarry."

"Ware, lad, ware," whispered Anthony excitedly,

fast growing interested in the sport; "see the quarry hath put in and Donald is at too high a pitch."

Sure enough the startled wild-goose, with forebodings of danger had " put in," as it was called — that is, made for security among the sedges at the water's edge.

"Nay, Anthony, nay, lad, 'tis quite right," Francis declared in a voice that tried to be steady ; "Donald doth but wait on a bit ; watch now, he will make his point ; Donald is too good a footer to miss his pitch."

"Ay, but look, the quarry hath put in still closer," said doubtful Anthony.

"Then must we serve the hawk, lad," declared hopeful Francis, and, darting across the stubble, both lads with loud cries flushed the now startled wild goose which, with a hoarse squawk, rose into a heavy flight.

Quick as thought the watchful tiercel swooped upon its prey.

"He binds; he binds!" cried Francis joyfully as the falcon pounced upon the gray goose and struck its cruel talons into head and neck.

Maddened with pain the big bird tried to shake off its captor, but to no purpose. The tiercel's talons sunk deeper into neck and brain and while the silver bells on the falcon's "bewits" tinkled musically, right at the edge of the stream with a lumbering fall dropped the big gray goose, dead from its wounds — the prize or "pelt" of Donald the tiercel.

"Well flown, well killed, good Donald!" shouted both the boys as they hurried to the spot. With a quick dash, Francis saved the "quarry" from slipping into the water, seized Donald's feet, slipped the plumed hood over its eyes, petted and praised it as he fastened its jess to his wrist and bidding Anthony take up the dead bird, plump and fat from its diet of September stubble, turned homeward well pleased with the morning's work.

But, ere they reached the gate of Gorhambury House, Francis, ready of ear and quick of eye, caught the sound of approaching horses and the gleam of color through the green of the Gorhambury beeches.

"Now what is this?" he cried; "why, who may

these be, Anthony? Hath our father, think you, any Michaelmas guests from court?"

"Nay, that I cannot say," replied his brother; "'twere wiser for us, say I, to stand aside a bit and see what we may see."

So, with falcon and quarry still in hand, the two lads drew to one side of the highway and awaited the coming cavalcade.

It drew nearer and yet nearer, and the boys could catch the gleam of head-piece and cuirass, of morris-pike and martel-top. Then the rich tints of the cloaks of the cavaliers, the flowing riding-habits of the ladies, and the burnished armor of the rear-guard, came into view while, central in the throng, guiding her milk-white horse with a grace and dignity of bearing that have become historic, rode a stately-looking lady whom the lads recognized at a glance, as their royal mistress and queen — Elizabeth of England.

"The queen, Anthony! it is the queen," cried young Francis Bacon, under his breath, and at once both boys dropped upon their knees so quickly that the nodding falcon on Francis's wrist very nearly lost his balance, while the big gray goose in Anthony's hand sprawled out before him on the ground.

The glittering cavalcade swept by, but, as the royal lady passed, her quick eye, always ready to detect and notice the sturdy youth of England, fell upon the two kneeling figures. She noted the big gray goose; she heard the tinkle of the falcon's bells.

"Odd's fish, Sir Nicholas, what have we here?" she cried gayly, touching with her riding whip a big, overgrown gentleman who rode at her bridle-rein. "Be these two youthful poachers, caught upon your own ground, my lord?"

The ponderous looking gentleman, who was none other than Sir Nicholas Bacon, Lord Chancellor of the Realm — or, rather, Lord Keeper of the Great Seal as the office was then styled — followed the Queen's laughing glance and recognized in the kneeling figures his own little lads.

"So please your grace," he said, "if these be poachers they be of mine own schooling. These be mine own two lads, Anthony and Francis."

"COME HITHER, LADS," SHE SAID.

"Why, man," cried Elizabeth still more gayly, "if that the good Lady Ann who schooled mine own dear brother hath two boys that have turned poachers, then is this our land of England in a sorry state. But methinks I have seen them before and can, I'll warrant me, trust their honest eyes. Are they not the young Cambridge students I have knowledge of? Come hither, lads," she said; and as the boys rose and came forward she stooped in her saddle and patted young Francis on his uncovered head.

"A brave young falconer I trow," said the Queen. "And how old are you, my lad?"

"So please your grace," answered the ready Francis, "just two years younger than your Majesty's glorious reign."*

It was a true courtier's reply and it pleased the Queen immensely.

"A right gracious lad, upon mine honor," she exclaimed, again stroking the uncovered head, "and what hath your falcon struck?"

"A stubble goose for your grace's Michaelmas,

---

* The boy's own words.

if but you will deign to accept it, madam," answered the boy.

"Of all things most acceptable, lad," answered the pleased Queen. "For what were Michaelmas without a goose and what goose could better serve for our Michaelmas than this one that so brave a lad hath taken? But stay," she added laughingly, "lest these officers of mine do find so rare a prize more suited to their own palates than their Queen's, keep you the quarry for me in trust, my lad, and even as your good father is Lord Keeper of our Great Seal, do you, Master Francis Bacon, be until we do relieve you of the office, Lord Keeper of our Michaelmas Goose. Wear you this in faith and fealty, my little Lord Keeper, as your badge of office," and always ready for a frolic the royal lady detached from her bridle rein one of the strips of cloth-of-gold that decorated it and flung it deftly across the shoulder of the delighted boy. Then, with quickened pace, the cavalcade rode onward toward Gorhambury gate.

Gorhambury House, with its oaks and beeches, its pillared front and "statlie gallarie," its gardens and orchards, was a most attractive place when Francis Bacon, the "little Lord Keeper," lived and played amid its birds and flowers, "old as a child," says his biographer, "growing younger as he grew in years."

It was to this residence of her favorite Lord Chancellor, the father of young Francis, that Queen Elizabeth had come in the course of her "progress," as it was called, from one portion of her domain to another. Selfish and avaricious, vindictive and high-tempered though she was, this greatest of England's queens could, when she pleased, be especially gracious and kindly.

And such seemed her mood on this Michaelmas visit to Gorhambury. Full of jests with her grave and ponderous Lord Keeper, and slyly trying to pierce the cold propriety of the Lady Ann, she was particularly friendly with young Francis whom she repeatedly addressed as "our little Lord Keeper" and plied with questions simply to hear his bright answers.

"Well, young Lord Keeper, and how is our Michaelmas goose?" was her inquiry as the lad came to her with grave and courtly obeisance on the fair Michaelmas morning — September 29, 1574.

"So please your grace, 'tis well," replied the boy, "and I can keep your royal trust till you do bid me render it up, though 'twere as long a time as the waits do pipe the watch."

"Why, lad, that is from Michaelmas Day to Maunday Thursday," laughed the Queen, "and sure 'twould be but a foul fowl ere that day. Methinks you would rather I had made you Lord Keeper of the royal games and bade you play them all, each day, from Barley-brake and All-hid to Cherrypit and Golf."

"And if you did, my liege," said the loyal young courtier, "I would gladly do it."

"I'll warrant me you would, lad," said the Queen sincerely; "but come now, what do you hope to achieve when you grow a man?"

"Something for the protection of your church and crown from papists and your grace's enemies," said the lad promptly; "something that may help the growing of this your realm of England and benefit the great world of men."

The Queen looked proudly at her loyal young subject who thus early gave promise of what his life-labor would be, and as she laid her hand upon his head she would doubtless have spoken tender and gracious words, but on that instant a great cry went up from the court-yard and queen and boy together looked down from the great square window. One glance told all, and with a cry of "O, that rascal Tib!" young Francis darted from the royal presence, and the Queen laughed heartily to see her Michaelmas goose dragged across the court-yard by a thievish black cat while scullion, turnspit and kitchen-boy ran shouting at its heels.

And now she sees young Francis with his trusty falcon join in the chase. Cat and goose are already scurrying over a heap of farm-yard muck. Off flies Donald, unhooded, from his master's wrist; with pitch and point he poises above the game and then with a sudden swoop down he darts and buries his sharp talons — not in the head of the thievish cat but in his old quarry the big gray goose, while wicked Tib dashes unharmed away to find refuge and remorse in the distant hay-rick near to the ample barns.

So Queen Elizabeth lost her Michaelmas goose, for what with cat and muck it was scarce fitted for the royal table. And though in mock anger she rated her little Lord Keeper roundly for his desertion of his trust she enjoyed the joke too thoroughly to let him long suffer mortification and soon rewarded his good intentions and his skill at falconry with pleasant words.

Fourteen years later another Michaelmas day saw a more fortunate goose on the royal table. For history reports that good Queen Bess was eating her Michaelmas goose when the joyous tidings of the defeat of the great Spanish Armada were brought to her; and the news, we may be sure, made most excellent sauce.

But at that time young Francis Bacon was no longer the "little Lord Keeper" of Gorhambury House. Grown a wise young man he was serving in the Parliament and preparing for those graver duties which were to make him, in time, the greatest of the Lord Chancellors of England and one of the world's most wonderful and learned men.

But the title which the Queen playfully gave in boyhood to her "little Lord Keeper" has clung to him quite as lastingly as did his later titles and honors; and his loyal service to his fickle but much loved Queen amply repaid that first lapse of duty when, through the wickedness of the thievish Tib, he lost his trust of Queen Elizabeth's Michaelmas goose.

XI.
HALLOW E'EN
A.D. 1340.

XI.

THE LITTLE DONNA JUANA.

[*An October Story of the Moors of Spain, and how the good Lord James of Douglas kept his Hallow E'en.* A. D. 1340.]

YOUNG Angus Leslie was delighted with Seville. That fair city by the Guadalquivir, so like an immense garden, with its flowers and sweet odors, its beautiful olive groves and orange trees, was as a dream of fairy-land to this bonny Scotch lad from the North.

For Angus was worn and weary from much travel; and after tossing about in a clumsy caravel on the Bay of Biscay and beating about Cape St. Vincent in a racking storm, he found the company of the young Spanish Dons and Donnas to be by far his most agreeable experience in his pilgrimage to Jerusalem.

Just what this pilgrimage to Jerusalem was, and just why it was undertaken are matters of historic interest. It so happened that when the great king Robert of Scotland, surnamed the Bruce — whom all boys and girls know as the hero of Bannockburn and the victim of a certain ridiculous and persistent spider — died in his palace at Cardross he bade his stanchest friend and companion-in-arms, Sir James Douglas, as he held his friendship sacred and his memory dear, to bear his heart, when he should be dead, to the city of Jerusalem and bury it in consecrated ground near to the Holy Sepulchre.

This seems to us a curious desire, but we must remember that those were far different days from these in which we live, filled with superstition and belief in good and ill luck, in dreams and omens.

And because the Bruce could not himself accomplish his great desire to go to Jerusalem to fight against the "Infidel," as the Saracen masters of Palestine were called, he felt, as he himself expressed it, that "since my body cannot go thither and accomplish that which my heart hath so desired, I have resolved to send my heart there, in place of my body, to fulfil my vow."

So the Lord Douglas, whom Scotchmen called for his knightly courage and courtesy "the good Lord James," and Englishmen for his daring and relentless warfare "the Black Douglas," prepared to carry out this last wish of his royal friend and master, and thus, sailing southward had he made the Spanish coast and reached the city of Seville, at that time the residence of the court of Alfonso XI. King of Leon and Castile.

Almost in the shadow of the snowy summits of the Sierra Morena and clustering on the banks of the winding Guadalquivir this old city of Southern Spain was for over five hundred years one of the most splendid cities of the Moorish conquerors. Built, so it was said, by Hercules,* rebuilt by Julius Cæsar, made splendid in architecture and civilization by the Western kalifs, reconquered by King Ferdinand the Saint, it was at the date of our story a Moorish city ruled by Christian lords, with windowless houses rich in Arabic decoration, narrow streets that shut out the heat

* Seville was, in fact, one of the colonies founded by the Phœnicians, the explorers and settlers of the ancient days.

of the sun, groves of olives and of oranges, fountains and gardens and all the luxuries of the splendid half-civilization of the most civilized of the followers of Mahomet — the Spanish Moors. A gay and splendid Spanish court now filled its palaces and its halls and everywhere was light and laughter, jest and song, the ring of armor, the flash of gorgeous color, the noise and motion of a city of soldiers in an age of wars. What wonder, then, that the band of Scottish knights and pilgrims found it a most attractive change from the colder northland and the treacherous sea! And what wonder that young Angus Leslie should have thoroughly enjoyed his new experience.

For Angus Leslie was a wide-awake lad always ready to enjoy his opportunities. He was one of the company of "twenty-six esquires, all comely young men of good family" who, the record assures us, followed the banner of Lord James of Douglas and the seven valiant knights who were his companions. And as with some of his new-found Spanish friends he spent the days in games and gossips in the magnificent gardens of the Al

Kasr, or House of Cæsar — the richly decorated Moorish palace in which was now assembled the court of the young King Alfonso — he listened to many a story of Moorish cunning and Spanish bravery, and told in return equally big stories of Scottish valor and the Douglas pluck. For young Angus was both kinsman and worshipper of the good Lord James.

But among all his Castilian acquaintances he found no more interested listener or companion than the little Donna Juana Manuel, the thirteen-year-old daughter of the brave Don Juan Manuel, warden of the Marches, or Moorish borders, and now valiantly defending, with the brave Don Alfonso Benavides, the little rocky city known as Tarifa, against the host of swarthy Moors of Morocco and of Fez, who had swarmed across from Africa for another conquest of the Christians.

The Donna Juana was a sprightly and highly attractive little Spanish maiden with the glossy hair and big dark eyes that all the girls of Southern Spain have had from the days of Don Roderick the Goth to now,

Every Scotch lad has — as in fact what boy has not — a love for the marvellous, and so has every Spanish girl. And as the stories of Scotch ways and Spanish lore passed between the two, Angus would tell of the ghosts and fairies, the spunkies and kelpies, the witches and brownies with which Scottish legend abounds, and he really regretted, so he assured the Donna Juana, much as he enjoyed Seville, he really regretted that he was not to be at home on Hallow E'en, for on that night of all others the Scot lads and lassies had "the jolliest and fearsomest times with the fairy folk of all the year. And what do you in Spain on Hallow E'en, my lady?" he inquired.

"O," said the girl, "we too do have a fearsome time. For we do take, when it is dark, figs and cakes, sweetmeats and nuts to the graveyard to buy off the djins and afrits and all the Infidel goblins that would otherwise break up the holy *velada** of the blessed saints."

"Nuts, say you?" cried young Angus, "then

---

* The veladas, or vigils, are kept in Spain with many gloomy ceremonies just before the season known as the "Day of All Saints."

there you are like us of the North. For sure Hallow E'en is nutcrack night with us, and 'tis said that if a girl does but place three nuts upon an over-hot hearth on Hallow E'en and doth name two after the lads she most favors, and one after herself, that one which doth first burn, with the one named for her, shall be the lad that she some day will wed."

The gay young Señorita clapped her hands joyously.

"Why, then will I too try that," she cried; "and as it were but scant courtesy to stranger guests to seem to prefer others before them, I will even name one of the nuts after you, Don Angus, and the other — the other — shall be — who? There be so many gallant youths in your Scottish train that I can scarcely make a second choice advisedly."

The page to Lord Douglas, schooled in courtly manners, bowed low in acknowledgment of the little lady's choice, and said, "Then try we another Scotch test, my lady. Let us pull kail — but ah, what know you of cabbage-stalks in sunny Spain? We must be content with orange sprouts."

So hand in hand, with closed eyes, according to true Scotch custom, the boy and girl wandered out into the sunlit garden of the Al Kasr and plucked the green shoots from the first orange tree they could grope against. These, according to Angus' direction, were placed above the curtained doorway of the noble Hall of the Ambassadors.

"Now then," said the lad, "he who first enters by that door shall be my hated rival. I will even now stand with targe and brand to dare him to the conflict for our lady's sake." And both laughed in glee as young Angus struck a most belligerent attitude before the rich doorway of that splendid Moorish hall.

But even as he did so the heavy curtain swayed and parted, and out into the marble *patio*, or open court, in which the young people were standing, stepped a noble-looking knight, tall and commanding in form, sparely built but pleasant-faced, with a merry eye and a gentle manner. His unhel-

SURPRISED BY THE HERO OF SEVENTY FIGHTS—THE GOOD LORD JAMES OF DOUGLAS.

meted head showed the crown of clustering black hair and the face without a scar, and both Angus and the Donna Juana somewhat shamefacedly drew back before the hero of seventy fights, the pride of Scottish chivalry, the good Lord James of Douglas.

The quick eye of the newcomer noted the start of surprise that his entrance caused, he noted the deep blush that sprang to the olive cheek of the Spanish maid, and he said gayly, " How now, my little lady, what new trick or mischief has yon young malapert been seeking to school you in ? "

" Nay, none, so please you, my lord," spake up Angus, " I did but seek to show the lady Juana some of our Hallow E'en devisings in bonny Scotland, and — "

" And so ye have pulled kail and roasted the nuts, have ye, laddie ? " cried Lord James, well versed in the customs of his homeland. " But you are over-hasty, Angus, lad," he added ; " sure 'tis full ten days to Hallow E'en and how may ye play Nutcrack Night before the time ? "

" Ah, but he did not that, my lord," brake in the

girl. "We did but place the kail above the doorway to gain choice of name, and even as we did so, why—"

"Why, in came I; is it so?" cried Lord James.

"And I am to be your choice then," as the Donna Juana nodded gayly; "the Black Douglas, as English folk do term me and affright their children withal — as gay a Scotch bachelor though, my lass, as ever danced over the border. I'll stand the test of the roasting, lady mine, but who, I pray, is my hated rival?"

"That am I, my lord," laughed Angus.

"Then, lad, we start fair," said the Lord James, and his face grew serious even in the midst of his laughing, "for sure we shall both be far from Seville on the Holy E'en, and the hot hearth shall give favor to neither. To-morrow, lad, doth the king's army march to meet the Infidel, and we who be rivals in this fair maid's test of faith shall be true and friendly page and lord when lances are couched and banners advanced."

And so indeed it was. The allied kings of Castile, of Arragon and of Portugal, joining force and arms against the "Infidel" were to march at once to the relief of the brave Spanish knights Manuel and de Benavides, who behind the walls of Tarifa were holding at bay the swarm of invading Moors.

At the time of our story Spain was divided between the Moorish kingdom of Granada and the Christian states of Castile, Arragon, Navarre and Portugal. Step by step the Christian knights were overcoming the Moorish possessions and the interest, which in earlier years had centered in the crusades against the Saracen conquerors of the Holy Land, now found a new field in the struggle between Christian and Moslem in Southern Spain.

It was this that had led the Lord Douglas to tarry at Seville; for as he sailed southward he had heard of the stress of Christian Spain from this latest invasion by the African Moors, and all the chivalric spirit of a Christian knight and a Scottish champion urged him to the belief that here, rather than in Jerusalem, was the "holy" land.

"Never shall it be said of me," he declared

when he heard of the critical condition of affairs, "that I turned away from the Cross in jeopardy."

Young Angus Leslie was overjoyed to hear that martial deeds were so speedily to be witnessed, for though enjoying himself greatly amid the pleasures of the Spanish court, like all wide-awake lads he welcomed anything that promised change or excitement.

But the little Donna Juana was still thinking of her Hallow-E'en test.

"But how shall I know," she asked with a merry laugh, "how shall I know that two such bitter rivals shall not live at feud, away from their lady's eyes? Pray you, sir knight, give me even now, as is the custom with our Castilian lords, some token of your willingness to keep truth with young Don Angus and true faith with me. Yon silver chain that lieth on your neck would be a fitting pledge."

Young Angus Leslie started uncomfortably at this thoughtless request of a merry girl, for he knew what token hung upon that glittering chain. But the Lord Douglas, with grave but tender face, drew the chain from beneath his velvet tunic and showed dangling at the end "a case of silver fine — beautifully enamelled."

"James of Douglas needs give no pledge for truth or faith, fair mistress," he said gently; "for he has that within this silvered case that keeps him ever leal. See, my children," he continued, as he pressed a spring upon the heart-shaped locket and disclosed its contents, "herein lies the heart of the grandest of kings and the noblest of men, the defence and comfort of Scotland, the kindest of masters and the tenderest of friends."

The young folks looked silently upon the sacred token — Angus awed and reverent, Juana touched but curious. It was the dried and shrivelled heart of King Robert Bruce.

"When I have that, my children," said the earl, "believe me, I am the stronger and the better at heart and need no pledge or token to cause me to keep faith with man or woman, lad or lass. So, fair mistress mine," he added more cheerily, "to whom I gayly pledge my faith for young Angus' safety from my jealous fears, if aught befall me e'er the Hallow E'en, remember that the heart of the Bruce guards well the Douglas faith, and that loyal love is alike for kings to honor and for maids to trust."

The Donna Juana's white kerchief fluttered her good-byes from the ladies' balcony above the king's gateway in the Al Kasr as the knights of Spain, of Portugal and of Scotland, rode out from princely Seville to do battle with the Moorish foe. Through the fairest of Spanish weather — the lovely days of October, in the year 1340 — the glittering cavalcade marched southward, Lord Douglas and his Scots holding the post of honor in the vanguard of the Christian host.

Young Angus Leslie rode near his chief, glorying in all this martial display and enjoying to the uttermost, as would any healthy boy, the inspiration of so grand a ride across the wooded plains, the fertile valleys, the olive-clad hills and the wild ravines of Southern Spain, until at last as he climbed the sharp slopes of the Sierra Nevada, dark with the shadows of its rocky cliffs and its stately evergreen oaks, a cry of delight sprang to his lips as his eye caught one of the world's noblest panoramas — the shores of two continents divided only by a narrow gulf and, beyond, the sparkling waters of the great White sea — the Baho el Abiad of the Moors, the Mediterranean of the Christians. Below, the embattled walls of Tarifa — the most southerly point of all Europe — crowned the rocky islet that jutted out into the narrow stretch of water which the Moors called Bab-ez-za-zak — "the gate of the narrow passage" — and which we of to-day know as the Straits of Gibraltar. Scarce twelve miles across rose the massive headlands of Africa and the white walls of Tangier, while at his feet on either side of a meagre little stream lay the plains of Salado fluttering with the tents and pennons of the Moorish host.

And great as was the lad's delight at the finest picture of rock and sea that he had looked upon since he had left his own bonny Scotland, greater still was his delight as he looked down upon the vast array of the "Infidel" invaders, hundreds of thousands strong, against whom he was soon to charge in the clash of battle.

Next day, on October 30, 1340, the trumpets sounded an advance and, with the Lord James of Douglas leading, the van and the allied kings riding at the centre and the rear, the Christian army sought to force a passage across the brackish Salado and through the swarming ranks of the Moors into beleaguered Tarifa.

It is not my purpose to describe the battle of the Salado. It was one of the bloodiest and most signal victories achieved in the long line of conflicts between the Crescent and the Cross. It stopped forever the tide of Moslem invasion in Western Europe, and it was one of the first steps toward the final overthrow of the Moorish power in Spain — an overthrow finally completed one hundred and fifty years later in the historic conquest of Granada by Ferdinand and Isabella, the royal patrons of Columbus.

For hours the battle waged. It was a strife of thousands against hundreds of thousands. Again and again the Moorish host seemed destined to overpower their Christian opponents by mere force of numbers.

Then the Douglas valor, greatest when most sorely pressed, rose supreme. "A Douglas, a Douglas. Rescue for the Cross!" rings his war-cry, and with a resistless sweep of lance and sword the Scottish knights charge against the foe. "So at the last," writes the old Scottish chronicler, Master John Barbour, "the Lord Douglas and they that were with him pressed the Saracens so fast that they wholly flee." And after the fleeing enemy galloped Lord James and ten of his knights, the hardest riders of the Scottish border.

The battle turns again. Once more the press of the enemy grew so dense that the banner of the Cross was in peril. Now one and now another of that gallant company fell beneath the arrows of the Moor. Then rose the Lord Douglas in his stirrups and taking from his neck the precious heart with which he had been entrusted, he threw it far before him into the very thickest of the press. "Now pass thou onward, noble heart, as thou was wont," he cried, "and we will follow thee, or die. Forward, forward, my brothers, the Bruce leads you as of yore!"

The Scots charged with furious onset following the heart of their king. De Benevides made a sudden sally from the town, the Spanish knights spurred across the Salado, the Infidel host turned in flight and the bloody field was won.

It was All Hallow E'en. Upon the victorious field of Salado, Christian and Saracen lay in mingling heaps of slain. Here and there the flaring torches of those who were searching for the lost lit up the scene, and with one of these parties went young Angus Leslie searching for the body of his lord. How different a Hallow E'en vigil from that which he he had laughingly described to the little Donna Juana.

At last the searchers recognize what they hoped yet feared to find, young Angus drops upon his knees with a bitter cry, while with sorrowing words the Scottish knights lift from the ground Lord James of Douglas, stark and dead. And there, beneath the body of their stricken lord, young Angus catches a gleam of silver in the flickering torchlight. All too well he knew that token, and with a mingling cry of joy and of sorrow he takes from its last victorious field, his master's charge and talisman — the heart of Robert Bruce.

War, boys and girls, has been one of the world's bitter necessities; for it is only by such strifes as these of system against system, and of race against race, that our civilization of to-day has been possible. But in the bloodiest wars some deed of valor, some act of generosity, of devotion or of faith, has lightened the gloom and horror of the time. And among the annals of knighthood no deed has ever shone brighter or more immortal than when on the bloody field of Salado the good Lord James of Douglas followed the lead of the kingly heart he had sworn to defend, and in the noblest of sacrifices kept his Hallow E'en.

XII.
THANKSGIVING-DAY
A.D. 1659.

XII.

PATEM'S SALMAGUNDI.

[A Thanksgiving-Day Story of Old New York in the time of Governor Stuyvesant. A. D. 1659.]

LITTLE Patem Onderdonk meant mischief. There was a snap in his eyes and a look on his face that were certain proof of this. I am bound to say however that there was nothing new or strange in this, for little Patem Onderdonk generally did mean mischief. Whenever any one's cow was found astray beyond the limits, or any one's bark gutter laid askew so that the roof-water dripped on the passer's head, or whenever the Dominie's dog ran howling down the Heeren Graaft with a battered pypken cover tied to his suffering tail, the goode vrouws in the neighborhood did not stop to wonder who could have done it; they simply raised both hands in a sort of injured resignation and exclaimed:

"*Ach so;* what's gone of Patem's Elishamet's Patem?"*

So you see little Patem Onderdonk was generally at the bottom of whatever of mischief was afoot in those last Dutch days of New Amsterdam on the island of Manhattan.

But this time he was conjuring a more serious bit of mischief than even he usually attempted. This was plain from the appearance of the startled but deeply interested faces of the half-dozen boys gathered around him on the Bridge.

"But I say, Patem," queried young Teuny Vanderbreets, who was always ready to second any of Patem's plans, "how can we come it over the dominie as you would have us?"

"So then, Teuny," cried Patem, in his highest key of contempt, "did your wits blow away with your hat out of Heer Snediker's nut-tree yesterday? Do not you know that the Heer Governor is at royal odds with Dominie Curtius because the skinflint old dominie will not pay the taxes due the town? Why, lad, the Heer Governor will back us up!"

---

* Peter's Elizabeth's Peter — one of the old Knickerbocker ways of distinguishing children by their parents' names.

"And why will he not pay the taxes, Patem?" asked Jan Hooglant, the tanner's son.

"Because he's a skinflint, I tell you," asserted Patem, "though I do believe he says that he was brought here from Holland as one of the Company's men, and ought not therefore pay taxes to the Company. That's what I did hear them say at the Stadt Huys this morning, and Heer Vanderveer, the schepen, said there, too, that Dominie Curtius was not worth one of the five hundred guilders which he doth receive for our teaching. And sure, if the Burgomaster and Schepens will have none of the old dominie, why then, no more will we who know how stupid are his lessons, and how his switch doth sting. So, hoy, lads, let's turn him out."

And with that little Patem Onderdonk gave Teuny Vanderbreets' broad back a sounding slap with his battered horn book and crying "Come on, lads," headed his mutinous companions on a race for the rickety little schoolhouse near the fort.

It was hard lines for poor Dominie Curtius all that day at school. The boys had never been so unruly; the girls never so inattentive. Rebellion seemed in the air, and the dominie, never a patient or gentle-mannered man, grew harsher and more exacting as the session advanced. His reign as master of the Latin School of New Amsterdam had not been a successful one, and his dispute with the town officers as to his payment of taxes had so angered him that, as Patem declared, " he seemed moved to avenge himself upon the town's children."

This being the state of affairs Dominie Curtius' mood this day was not a pleasant one, and the school exercises had more to do with the whipping horse and the birch twigs than with the horn book and the Latin conjugations.

The boys, I regret to say, were hardened to this, because of much practice, but when the dominie, enraged at some fresh breach of rigid discipline, glared savagely over his big spectacles and then swooped down upon pretty little Antje Adrianse who had done nothing whatever, the whole school broke into open rebellion. Horn books, and every possible missile that the boys had at hand went flying at the master's head, and the young rebels, led on by Patem and Teuny, charged down upon the unprepared dominie, rescued trembling little Antje from his clutch, and then one and all rushed pell-mell from the school with shouts of triumph and derision.

But when the first flush of their victory was over, the boys realized that they had done a very daring and risky thing. It was no small matter in those days of stern authority and strict home government for girls and boys to resist the commands of their elders; and to run away from school was one of the greatest of crimes. So they all looked at Patem in much anxiety.

"Well," cried several of the boys almost in a breath, "and now what shall we do, Patem? You have us in a pretty fix."

Patem waved his hand like a young Napoleon.

"*Ach;* ye are all cowards," he cried shrilly. "What will we *do?* Why, then we will but do as if we were burgomasters and schepens — as we will be some day. We will to the Heer Governor straight, and lay our demands before him."

Well, well; this *was* bold talk! The Heer Governor! Not a boy in all New Amsterdam but would sooner face a gray wolf in the Sapokanican woods than the Heer Governor Stuyvesant.

"So then, Patem Onderdonk," they cried, "you may do it yourself, for, good faith, we will not."

"Why," said Jan Hooglant, "why, Patem, the Heer Governor will have us rated soundly over the ears for daring such a thing; and we will all catch more of it when we get home. Demand of the Heer Governor indeed! Why, boy, you must be crazy!"

But Patem was not crazy. He was simply determined; and, at last, by threats and arguments and coaxing words he gradually won over a half-dozen of the boldest spirits to his side and, without more ado, started with them to interview the Heer Governor.

But, quickly as they acted, the schoolmaster was still more prompt in action. Defeated and deserted by his scholars, Dominie Curtius had raged about the schoolroom for a while, spluttering angrily in mingled Dutch and Polish, and then, clapping his broad black hat upon his head, marched straight to the fort to lay his grievance before the Heer Governor.

The Heer Petrus Stuyvesant, Director General for the Dutch West India Company in their colony of New Netherlands, walked up and down the Governor's chamber in the fort at New Amsterdam wofully perplexed. The Heer Governor was not a patient man, and a combination of annoyances were hedging him about and making his government of his island province anything but pleasant work.

The "malignant English" of the Massachusetts and Hartford colonies were pressing their claim to the ownership of the New Netherlands, just as, to the south, the settlers on Lord De La Ware's patent were also doing; the "people called Quakers" whom the Heer Governor had publicly whipped for heresy and sent a-packing were spreading their "pernicious doctrine" through Long Island and other outer edges of the colony, and the Indians around Esopus, the little settlement which the province had planted midway on the Hudson between New Amsterdam and Beaverwyck (now Albany) were growing restless and defiant. Thump, thump, thump, across the floor went the wooden leg with its silver bands, and with every thump the Heer Governor grew still more puzzled and angered. For the Heer Governor could not bear to have things go wrong.

Suddenly, with scant ceremony and but the apology of a request for admittance, there came into the Heer Governor's presence, the Dominie Doctor Alexander Carolus Curtius, master of the Latin School.

"Here is a pretty pass, Heer Governor," he cried excitedly. "My pupils of the Latin School have turned upon me in revolt and have deserted me in a body."

"*Ach;* then you are rightly served for a craven and a miser, sir," burst out the angry Governor, turning savagely upon the surprised schoolmaster.

This was a most unexpected reception for Doctor and Dominie Curtius. But, as it happened, the Heer Governor Stuyvesant was just now particularly vexed with the objectionable Dominie.

At much trouble and after much solicitation on his part the Heer Governor had prevailed upon his superiors and the proprietors of the province, the Dutch West India Company, to send from Holland a schoolmaster or "rector" for the children of their town of New Amsterdam, and the Company had sent over Dominie Curtius.

The Heer Governor had entertained great hopes of what the new schoolmaster was to do, and now to find him a subject of complaint from both the parents of the scholars and the officials of the town, made the hasty Governor doubly dissatisfied. The dominie's intrusion, therefore, at just this stage of all his perplexities gave the Heer Governor a most convenient person on whom to vent his bad feelings.

"Yes, sirrah, a craven and a miser," continued the angry Governor, stamping upon the floor with both wooden leg and massive cane; "you, who can neither govern our children or pay your just dues to the town, can be no fit master for our youth. No words, sirrah, no words," he added as the poor dominie tried to put in a word in his defence, "no words, sir; you are discharged from further labor in this province. I will see that one who can rule wisely and pay his just dues shall be placed here in your stead."

Protests and appeals, explanations and arguments were of no avail. When the Heer Governor Stuyvesant said a thing, he meant it, and it was useless for any one to hope for a change. The unpopular Dominie Curtius must go — and go he did.

But, as he left, the delegation of boys, headed by young Patem Onderdonk, came into the fort and sought to interview the Heer Governor.

The sentry at the door would have sent them off without further ado, but, hearing their noise, the Heer Governor himself came to the door.

"So, so, young rapscallions," he cried, "you too must needs disturb the peace and push yourself forward into public quarrels. Get you gone! I will have none of your words. Is it not enough that I must needs send the schoolmaster a-packing, without being worried by such graceless young varlets as you."

"And hath the Dominie Curtius gone indeed, Heer Governor?" Patem dared to ask.

"Hath he, hath he, boy!" echoed the Governor, turning upon his audacious young questioner with uplifted cane. "Said I not so, and would you dare doubt my word, rascal? Begone from the fort, all of you, ere I do put you all in limbo, or send word to your good folk to give you the floggings you do no doubt all so richly deserve."

Discretion is the better part of valor, and the boyish delegation hastily withdrew. But when once they were safely out of hearing of the Heer Governor, beyond the Land Gate at the Broad Way, they took breath and indulged in a succession of boyish shouts.

"And that doth mean no school too," cried young Patem Onderdonk, flinging his cap in air. "Huzzoy for that, lads; huzzoy for that!"

And the "huzzoys" came with right good will from every boy of the group.

Within less than a week the whole complexion of affairs in that little island city was entirely changed. Both the Massachusetts and the Maryland claimants ceased, for a time at least, their unfounded demands. A treaty at Hartford settled the disputed question of boundary lines, and the Maryland Governor declared that "he had not intended to meddle with the government at Manhattan." Added to this, Sewackenamo, chief of the Esopus Indians, came to the fort at New Amsterdam and "gave the right hand of friendship" to the Heer Governor, and by the interchange of presents a treaty of peace was ratified. So, one by one, the troubles of the Heer Governor melted away, his brow became clear and, partaking of the universal satisfaction," so says the historian, " he proclaimed a day of general thanksgiving."

Thanksgiving in the colonies was a matter of almost yearly occurrence. Since the first Thanksgiving Day on American shores, when, in 1621, the Massachusetts colony, at the request of Governor Bradford, rejoiced "after a special manner after we had gathered the fruit of our labors," the observance of days of thanksgiving for mercies and benefits had been frequent. But the day itself dates still further back. The States of Holland after establishing their freedom from Spain had, in the year 1609, celebrated their deliverance from tyranny "by thanksgiving and hearty prayers," and had thus really first instituted the custom of an official thanksgiving. And the Dutch colonists in America followed the customs of the Fatherland quite as piously and fervently as did the English colonists.

So, when the proclamation of the Heer Governor Stuyvesant for a day of Thanksgiving was made known, in this year of mercies 1659, all the town folk of New Amsterdam made ready to keep it.

But young people are often apt to think that the world moves for them alone. The boys of this little Dutch town at the mouth of the Hudson were no different from other boys, and cared less for treaties and Indians and boundary questions than for their own matters. They therefore concluded that the Heer Governor had proclaimed a thanksgiving because, as young Patem Onderdonk declared, "he had gotten well rid of Dominie Curtius and would have no more schoolmasters in the colony."

"And so, lads," cried the exuberant young Knickerbocker, "let us wisely celebrate the Thanksgiving; I will even ask the mother to make for me a rare salmagundi which we lads, who were so rated by the Heer Governor, will ourselves give to him as our Thanksgiving offering — for the Heer Governor, so folk do say, doth rarely like the salmagundi."

Now the salmagundi was (to some palates) a most appetizing mixture, compounded of salted mackerel, or sometimes of chopped meat, seasoned with oil and vinegar, pepper and raw onions — not an altogether attractive dish to read of, but welcome and dearly loved by many an old Knickerbocker even up to a recent date. Its name too, as some of you bright boys and girls doubtless know, furnished the title for one of the works of Washington Irving, best loved of all the Knickerbockers.

Thanksgiving Day came around, and so did Patem's salmagundi, as highly seasoned and appetizing a one as the Goode Vrouw Onderdonk could make.

The lengthy prayers and lengthier sermon of good Dominie Megapolensis in the Fort Church were over and the Thanksgiving dinners were very nearly ready when, up to the Heer Governor's house, came a half-dozen boys, with Patem Onderdonk at their head bearing a neatly covered dish.

Patem had well considered and formed in his mind what he deemed just the speech of presentation to please the Heer Governor, but when the time came to face that awful personage, his valor and his eloquence alike began to ooze away.

And, it must be confessed, the Heer Governor Stuyvesant did not understand boys, nor did he particularly favor them. He was hasty and overbearing though high-minded, loyal and brave, but he never could "get on" with the ways and pranks of boys.

And, as for the boys themselves, when once they stood in the presence of the greatest dignitary in the province, Patem's ready tongue seemed to cleave to the roof of his mouth, and he hummed and hawed and hesitated until the worthy Heer Governor lost patience and broke in —

"Well, well, boys; what is the stir. Speak

quick if at all; for when a man's dinner waiteth he hath scant time for stammering boys."

Then Patem spoke up.

"Heer Governor," he said, "the boys hereabout, remembering your goodness in sending away our most pestilential master, the Dominie Curtius, and in proclaiming a Thanksgiving for his departure and for the ending of our schooling"—

"What, what, boy!" cried the Heer Governor, "art crazy then, or would you seek to make sport of me, your governor? Thanksgiving for the breaking-up of school! Out on you for a set of malapert young knaves! Do you think the world goeth but for your pleasures alone? Why, this is ribald talk. I made no Thanksgiving for your convenience, rascals, but because that the Lord in his grace hath relieved the town from danger"—

"Of which, Heer Governor," broke in the most impolitic Patem, "we did think the Dominie Curtius and his school were part. And so we have brought to you this salmagundi as our Thanksgiving offering to you for thus freeing us of a pest and a sorrow"—

THE BOYS PRESENT THE SALMAGUNDI TO THE HEER GOVERNOR STUYVESANT.

"How now, how now, sirrah," again came the interruption from the scandalized Heer Governor when he could recover from his surprise, "do you then dare to call your schooling a pest and a sorrow? Why, you graceless young varlets, I do not seek to free you from schooling? I do even now seek to bring you speedily the teaching you do so much stand in need of. Even now, within the week forthcoming, the good Dominie Luyck, the tutor of mine own household, will see to the training and teaching of this town, and so I will warrant, to the flogging, too, of all you sad young rapscallions who even now by this your wicked talk do show your need both of teaching and of flogging."

And then, forgetful of the boys' Thanksgiving offering and in high displeasure at what he deemed their wilful and deliberate ignorance, the Heer Governor turned the delegation into the street and hastened back to his waiting dinner.

"*Ach, so,*" cried young Teuny Vanderbreets, as the disgusted and disconsolate six gathered in the roadway and looked at one another, rueful and disconsolate, "here is a fine mix-up — a regular salmagundi, Patem Onderdonk, and no question. And you did say that this Thanksgiving was all our work. Out upon you, say I! Here are we to be saddled with a worse master than before. Hermanus Smeeman did tell me that Nick Stuyvesant did tell him that the Dominie Luyck is a most hard and worryful master."

There was a universal groan of disappointment and disgust, and then Patem said philosophically:

"Well, lads, what's done is done, and what is to be will be. Let us eat the salmagundi anyhow and cry: Confusion to Dominie Luyck."

And they did eat it, then and there, for indigestion had no terror to those lads of hardy stomachs.

But as for the toast of "Confusion to Dominie Luyck," that came to naught. For Dominie Ægidius Luyck proved a most efficient and skilful teacher. Under his rule the Latin School of New Amsterdam became famous throughout the colonies, so that scholars came to it for instruction from Beaverwyck and South River and even from distant Virginia.

So the Thanksgiving of the boys of New Amsterdam became a day of mourning, and Patem's influence as a leader and an oracle suffered sadly for a while.

Five years after, on a sad Monday morning in September, 1664, the little city was lost to the Dutch West India Company and, spite of the efforts and the protests of its sturdy Governor, the red, white and blue banner of the Netherlands gave place to the flag of England. And when that day came the young fellows who then saw the defeat and disappointment of the Heer Governor Stuyvesant, were not so certain that Patem Onderdonk was wrong when he claimed that it was all a just and righteous judgment on the Heer Governor for his refusal of the boys' request for no school, and for his treatment of them on that sad Thanksgiving Day when he so harshly rebuked their display of gratitude and lost forever his chance to partake of Patem's Salmagundi.

www.ingramcontent.com/pod-product-compliance
Lightning Source LLC
Chambersburg PA
CBHW031959230426
43672CB00010B/2212